DAVID SIMON
HENRIETTA PALMER
JAN RIISE

T0335080

COMPARATIVE URBAN RESEARCH FROM THEORY TO PRACTICE

Co-Production For Sustainability

POLICY PRESS **SHORTS** POLICY & PRACTICE

First published in Great Britain in 2020 by

Policy Press
University of Bristol
1-9 Old Park Hill
Bristol
BS2 8BB
UK
t: +44 (0)117 954 5940
pp-info@bristol.ac.uk
www.policypress.co.uk

North America office:
Policy Press
c/o The University of Chicago Press
1427 East 60th Street
Chicago, IL 60637, USA
t: +1 773 702 7700
f: +1 773-702-9756
sales@press.uchicago.edu
www.press.uchicago.edu

© Policy Press 2020

The digital PDF version of this title is available Open Access and distributed under the terms of the Creative Commons Attribution-NonCommercial 4.0 license (http://creativecommons. org/licenses/by-nc/4.0/) which permits adaptation, alteration, reproduction and distribution for non-commercial use, without further permission provided the original work is attributed. The derivative works do not need to be licensed on the same terms.

British Library Cataloguing in Publication Data
A catalogue record for this book is available from the British Library

Library of Congress Cataloging-in-Publication Data
A catalog record for this book has been requested

ISBN 978-1-4473-5312-6 (paperback)
ISBN 978-1-4473-5407-9 (ePub)
ISBN 978-1-4473-5409-3 (ePdf)

The right of David Simon, Henrietta Palmer and Jan Riise to be identified as editors of this work has been asserted by them in accordance with the Copyright, Designs and Patents Act 1988.

All rights reserved: no part of this publication may be reproduced, stored in a retrieval system, or transmitted in any form or by any means, electronic, mechanical, photocopying, recording, or otherwise without the prior permission of Policy Press.

The statements and opinions contained within this publication are solely those of the editors and contributors and not of the University of Bristol or Policy Press. The University of Bristol and Policy Press disclaim responsibility for any injury to persons or property resulting from any material published in this publication.

Policy Press works to counter discrimination on grounds of gender, race, disability, age and sexuality.

Cover design by Dave Worth
Front cover image: Jan Riise
Printed and bound in Great Britain by CMP, Poole
Policy Press uses environmentally responsible print partners

Contents

List of figures and tables

Figures

Tables

List of acronyms and abbreviations

CBO	community-based organisation
CTLIP	Cape Town Local Interaction Platform
GOLIP	Gothenburg Local Interaction Platform
KLIP	Kisumu Local Interaction Platform
LIP	Local Interaction Platform
MUF	Mistra Urban Futures
NUA	New Urban Agenda
QME	quality monitoring and evaluation
SDGs	Sustainable Development Goals
SKLIP	Skåne Local Interaction Platform
SMLIP	Sheffield–Manchester Local Interaction Platform
SWM	solid waste management
TOD	transport-oriented development

Notes on the editors

David Simon is Professor of Development Geography at Royal Holloway, University of London and was on secondment from 2014 to 2019 as Director of Mistra Urban Futures, Gothenburg. He specialises in development–environment issues, with particular reference to cities, climate change and sustainability, and the relationships between theory, policy and practice, on all of which he has published extensively. He is author of *Holocaust Escapees and Development: Hidden histories* (Zed Books, 2019) editor of *Rethinking Sustainable Cities* (Policy Press, 2016) and *Key Thinkers on Development* (Routledge, 2019), and co-editor of *Urban Planet* (Cambridge University Press, 2018). His extensive research experience spans sub-Saharan Africa, tropical Asia, the UK, the USA and Sweden.

Henrietta Palmer is an architect and researcher. She was Artistic Professor of Urban Design at Chalmers University of Technology, Gothenburg, and was Deputy Scientific Director at Mistra Urban Futures from 2015 to 2019, with a particular engagement in methodologies for transdisciplinary research, also developing a PhD course for transdisciplinary research. From 2005 to 2015, she was Professor of Architecture at the Royal Institute of Art, Stockholm, where she designed and conducted the transdisciplinary post-master's programme in resources, focusing on urban challenges with contextual studies across a number of cities globally. Her key research focus concerns just urban transformation processes stemming from social-spatial practices.

Jan Riise was Engagement Manager at Mistra Urban Futures from 2016 to 2019. Jan has been working in the interface between science and society for almost three decades and is particularly interested in the participation of other actors, such as citizens and people from the public and private sectors. He was the Director of the European Science Engagement Association from 2013 to 2015 and a member of the Scientific Committee of the global network Public Communication of Science and Technology, and engaged in several other international organisations in the field.

Notes on contributors

Nils Björling is an architect and Senior Lecturer in Urban Design and Planning in Architecture and Civil Engineering at Chalmers University of Technology, Gothenburg. Nils' teaching and research seek to develop theory and methods to increase the interplay between local, municipal and regional planning in order to support the design practice to manage challenges caused by uneven geographical development and to include a broader field of resources and actors in the planning process.

Sylvia Croese is an urban sociologist and researcher at the African Centre for Cities at the University of Cape Town, South Africa. From 2017 to 2019 she worked as an embedded researcher in the City of Cape Town as part of the Mistra Urban Futures research project entitled Implementing the New Urban Agenda and the Sustainable Development Goals: Comparative Urban Perspectives.

Elma Durakovic has a background in economics, specifically environmental economics, from the University of Gothenburg. From 2019 she has been Acting Director at the Gothenburg Platform within Mistra Urban Futures. Since 2017, she has also been project lead for the comparative project Transport and Sustainable Urban Development, a collaboration between Gothenburg, Kisumu and Cape Town. Her interest is in transdisciplinary research and knowledge co-production and how to organise these types of collaborations.

Kristina Diprose is a social researcher whose recent projects have focused on public perceptions of climate change, the intersection of arts and social research, and local implementation of the United Nations Sustainable Development Goals. Her work is published in various human geography journals and she is the lead author of *Climate Change, Consumption and Intergenerational Justice: Lived Experiences in China, Uganda and the UK* (Bristol University Press, 2019).

Mirek Dymitrow holds a PhD in human geography from the University of Gothenburg, where he was a research fellow until December 2019. He is now a postdoctoral fellow at Lund University. He also works as research co-ordinator at Chalmers University of Technology. His research interests include social psychology and sociology of science with a focus on conceptual change and inertia, as well as problems and causes of social deprivation in the face of overarching sustainability goals.

Gareth Haysom is a researcher at the African Centre for Cities at the University of Cape Town, working in the African Centre for Cities' urban food systems research cluster. His work focuses on urbanisation in the global South with a specific interest in African cities. Gareth's contribution to this volume emerged from a comparative urban food system engagement between Mistra Urban Futures researchers in four very different cities, drawing on different contextual experiences and food system challenges and needs.

Karin Ingelhag is a project manager within business development, and a former educator. Karin's current engagements include running the European Union project Urban Rural Gothenburg as well as co-ordinating research in collaboration between the City of Gothenburg and Chalmers University of

Technology. Karin's academic background in psychology and behavioural sciences recurs in her ongoing work with sustainability transitions.

Eva Maria Jernsand holds a PhD in Business Administration from the School of Business, Economics and Law, which is part of the University of Gothenburg, and is a researcher in marketing at the School of Business, Economics and Law at the University of Gothenburg, and affiliated with the Centre for Tourism at the same university. Her research interests include place branding, participation, transdisciplinary research, innovation, design and sustainable tourism development. Eva Maria's work is published in journals such as *Place Branding and Public Diplomacy*, *Scandinavian Journal of Hospitality and Tourism*, *Action Research* and *Tourism Recreation Research*.

Magnus Johansson has a PhD in pedagogy from Lund University. He divides his time between the Department of Urban Studies, Malmö University, where he works as Assistant Professor in Environmental Studies, and the Research Institutes of Sweden, where he works as a senior researcher, affiliated to the unit of sustainable communities.

Shelley Kotze holds a PhD in human geography from the University of Gothenburg. She previously held the post of project assistant at Urban Rural Gothenburg's Research Forum. Her research interests include place keeping, immigrant integration and public green space interactions, and the polarisation of gender.

Helena Kraff has a PhD in design, and is a researcher in design at the Faculty of Fine, Applied and Performing Arts at the University of Gothenburg. Her main research interests include participatory design and transdisciplinary research methodology. Her thesis identifies and critically explores a number of challenges related to participatory research practices in Kisumu. She has published in international journals and edited books, and written reports in the areas of participatory design, tourism, place branding and transdisciplinary research.

Barry Ness was, until December 2019, the Director of the Skåne Local Interaction Platform (SKLIP) for Mistra Urban Futures. He is also a project researcher on the Mistra Urban Futures solid waste management comparative project. Barry is Associate Professor in Sustainability Science at the Centre for Sustainability Science at Lund University, where his current research interests focus on promoting and understanding sustainability in the craft beer sector through bottom-up, participatory approaches. Past research themes have included sustainability assessment, the diffusion of simple, more sustainable innovations in Africa, and large land acquisitions in Africa.

Joakim Nordqvist holds a PhD in environmental and energy systems studies and is affiliated to the Institute for Sustainable Urban Development at Malmö University. He also holds a position as climate strategist at the Environment Department of the City of Malmö, focusing on partnerships for sustainability action and on transdisciplinary learning. His research interests home in on challenges of sustainability in built environments.

Michael Oloko is a senior lecturer, researcher and Dean of the School of Engineering and Technology at Jaramogi Oginga Odinga University of Science and Technology. He is also the Deputy Director for research at Kisumu Local Interaction Platform. He holds a PhD in agricultural engineering from Egerton University. His current research interests include environmental engineering, integrated water resources management, renewable energy technology, urban agriculture and waste management.

Lillian Omondi is a sociologist with a PhD in sociology and lectures at Maseno University's Department of Sociology and

Anthropology, Kenya. Her research interests include social capital and its influence on community action, migration and migrant networks, engendering research and community action, and community-led climate change adaptation. Her recent publications include, with Merritt Polk and Mary Aswan Ochieng, 'Social Capital and Climate Change Perception in the Mara River Basin, Kenya' (*Research on Humanities and Social Sciences* 5(12), 2015).

Beth Perry is Professorial Fellow at the Urban Institute at the University of Sheffield. Her research focuses on processes and practices of urban transformation, co-productive urban governance, citizen participation and the just city. Beth oversees a collaborative programme of work between academics, individuals and organisations supporting progressive social, spatial and environmental change in the North of England. Recent books include *Reflexivity: The Essential Guide* (Sage Publications, 2017), *Cities and the Knowledge Economy* (Routledge, 2018) and *Cultural Intermediaries Connecting Communities: Revisiting Approaches to Cultural Engagement* (Policy Press, 2019).

Erica Righard is Associate Professor at the Department of Social Work and the Malmö Institute for Studies of Migration, Diversity and Welfare, Malmö University. From 2018 to 2019, she co-ordinated the International Migration and Urban Development Panel at SKLIP. She also co-co-ordinated the Mistra Urban Futures comparative project on Migration and Urban Development. Her research is multidisciplinary and mainly focused on the intersection of international migration and social protection. She is a member of the International Migration, Integration and Social Cohesion network's Standing Committee on Transnationalism, and chaired Nordic Migration Research from 2015 to 2018.

Bert Russell is an action researcher with a focus on municipalist politics, economic democracy and the commons, with publications in journals such as *Antipode*, *City* and *Area*. He is also co-founder of the UK's Municipal Action, Research and Advocacy Network and a committed public intellectual, with articles published on websites such as openDemocracy, Red Pepper, Novara Media, CityMetric and ROAR Magazine, and in *New Internationalist*.

Tarun Sharma is co-founder of Nagrika (Sanskrit for 'citizen'), a social enterprise addressing the issues of small cities and their citizens. Nagrika creates knowledge for and from small cities and uses this knowledge to enable better governance and enable citizen-led transformation in these cities. Tarun is based in Dehradun, India. He is the lead researcher for Shimla on the New Urban Agenda and Sustainable Development Goals Comparative Urban Perspectives project.

Rike Sitas is fascinated by the intersection of art, culture and heritage in urban life, and straddles the academic world of urban studies and creative practice. Of particular interest is how artful practices produce new knowledge of and action in cities. Rike is a researcher at the African Centre for Cities at the University of Cape Town. In addition to being the Local Interaction Platform co-ordinator for Mistra Urban Futures, her projects include Cultural Heritage and Just Cities; Whose Heritage Matters; Power of Place; Knowledge Transfer Programme and Knowledge Exchange; Realising Just Cities; and UrbanAfrica.Net.

Warren Smit is the Manager of Research at the African Centre for Cities, University of Cape Town, and was the Director of the Mistra Urban Futures Cape Town Local Interaction Platform from 2016 to 2019. He has a PhD in urban planning and has been a researcher on urban issues for over 25 years. His main areas of research include urban governance, urban health and housing policy, with a particular focus on African cities.

Sandra C. Valencia is an interdisciplinary researcher with a PhD in sustainability science from Lund University, a BSc in physics and an MSc in development management. Until December 2019, she led a comparative research project on city-level implementation of Agenda 2030 in seven cities on four continents at Mistra Urban Futures, Chalmers University of Technology, Gothenburg. She has worked as a research scientist at NASA Goddard Space Flight Center for the Micro-pulse Lidar Network project on atmospheric data. She also worked for several years developing and managing climate change adaptation projects in Latin America and the Caribbean at the Inter-American Development Bank.

Ileana Versace is an architect at the School of Architecture, Design and Urbanism, University of Buenos Aires (FADU, UBA), where she specialises in history and critics of architecture and urbanism. She is also a PhD student and Adjunct Professor, History of Architecture at FADU, UBA. Her other roles include main researcher, Institute of American Art and Aesthetical Research 'Mario J. Buschiazzo' and General Co-ordinator, Department of International Programs, both at FADU, UBA; and General Co-ordinator in Buenos Aires, Observatory on Latin America, The New School, New York.

ONE

Introduction: from unilocal to comparative transdisciplinary urban co-production of knowledge

David Simon, Jan Riise and Henrietta Palmer

Co-production as a research approach

Co-production of knowledge as an approach has evolved since the 1970s. The objective has been to bring different stakeholder groups together in an attempt to improve outcomes, whether of services or research, and their legitimacy and to overcome often longstanding antagonisms and wide asymmetries of power by working or researching together (Jasanoff, 2004; Joshi and Moore, 2004; Mitlin, 2008; Polk, 2015a).

Co-production is generally seen as good for society, at least in relevant fields of research, as co-production is more equitable and includes more diverse voices and perspectives than traditional research (Durose et al, 2018). In the particular context of sustainable urban development, the terms co-production, co-creation and co-design have emerged to inform new expectations of project design, where the beneficiaries or users of a given intervention also participate in its design, research and implementation. Co-creation and co-design are gaining currency because they draw attention to the joint definition of shared problems and the design of an appropriate methodology, as well as undertaking the actual research, whereas co-production is sometimes used to denote only the actual research being undertaken jointly, on a design and methodology formulated by one or two participants, usually academic researchers. In this book, for convenience, we use co-production as a shorthand term to embrace all these variants.

The co-production approach to both research and service provision is now widely used in diverse situations in both the global South and North. In development contexts, co-production is often presented as a means of identifying and incorporating local and/or traditional forms of knowledge into development, thus moving beyond the problematic a priori valorisation of either local/traditional or generally Western scientific knowledge. However, this is far from straightforward in practice and many questions regarding how to integrate knowledge remain to be resolved, as will emerge in several chapters in this book.

Essentially, the many modes of co-production constitute more sustained and coherent forms of the diverse participatory research and consultation methods[1] developed to engage with local communities, research subjects, or the intended beneficiaries of development or service investments. There is no clear boundary between co-production and participation – when the intention is to increase diverse stakeholders' active involvement and effective power within the process concerned – in order to increase both the degree of democracy in the process, and confidence in and the legitimacy of the outputs and outcomes, and to diversify epistemically the knowledge produced. Indeed, for instance, participatory budgeting, of the kind initiated in Porto Alegre (Brazil) and subsequently applied in diverse cities (Cabannes, 2004, 2015), has many attributes of co-production, but even so is not immune from ossification and bureaucratisation over time, which have given rise to criticisms and loss of legitimacy.

Globally, co-production has most commonly involved local authorities and other public sector institutions engaging with residents and organised community groups, often in relation to service provision. This derives from initial work by Roger Parks and colleagues including Elinor and Victor Ostrom (1981) and the diverse forms have recently been characterised as constituting a typology in terms of the degree of participation by service users (Brandsen and Honingh, 2016; see also Polk, 2015a, 2015b; Durose and Richardson, 2016; Wolf and Mahaffey, 2016). Nevertheless, nowadays the term co-production also applies to diverse forms, partnerships and applications of research, including, for instance, in relation to global change and peri-urban disaster risk reduction (Mauser et al, 2013; Schaer and Komlavi Hanonou, 2017) and the health sector. The literature demonstrates how challenging, time-consuming and sometimes unpredictable genuine co-production of knowledge and understanding can be in terms of outcomes. Perhaps unsurprisingly, therefore, the now-considerable literature on co-production of research around the world is overwhelmingly conceptual or based on research in one location rather than being comparative across locations. It also tends to assume – usually implicitly since these issues are not always addressed – that power differentials among co-production participants and their respective institutions can be overcome and that consensus can be achieved through sustained negotiation. In practice, as will emerge through the pages of this book, these assumptions frequently do not hold.

Co-produced research, like the co-production of services, can sometimes also be transdisciplinary. Although this latter term may be used synonymously with interdisciplinary to refer to the crossing of academic disciplines, here we adopt the usage denoting the collaboration of academics and practitioner/practice-oriented researchers from different disciplines and/or backgrounds. Transdisciplinary co-produced research,

then, emphasises inclusiveness and iterative, deliberative negotiation as the mechanism for building shared understandings
as a precondition for making progress jointly. As such, it
involves a team made up of practitioners and academics, creating a fundamentally different epistemology of social science
knowledge production from the conventional linear, positivist and expert-led model that still underpins most urban
research worldwide. The existence and relevance of 'different
knowledges', including those of indigenous and local communities, have been acknowledged, hence understanding that
capacity and legitimacy are crucial components of transitional
or transformational actions towards sustainability at all levels.

Urban research has become a particularly important field
for experimentation and innovation in the co-production
of knowledge. Cities around the world are key actors in the
struggle against global climate change, as well as in the development of urban social sustainability, which is defined in terms
of social equity and community sustainability (Dempsey et al,
2011). These concerns also underpin the research of Mistra
Urban Futures and in particular the Realising Just Cities
framework (discussed later in the chapter), which has guided
our research agenda for the period 2016–19, including the
comparative transdisciplinary co-production initiatives that
form the subject of this book. Although time-consuming and
less predictable than conventional research, co-production
is an approach that may create both legitimacy and action
through new policies and local strategies (Simon et al, 2018),
because it builds a shared sense of collective ownership of
the outcomes by virtue of the whole research process being
a joint experience.

The importance of such an approach is given added relevance by the current global societal challenges and international agendas for sustainable development, which explicitly
recognise the importance of co-production among the multiple stakeholders and levels of governance institutions, both

intra- and internationally. The next section summarises these agendas briefly.

Global challenges and the urban

With *Homo sapiens* now a predominantly urban species, urbanisation and globalisation are changing the world and will continue to do so for decades to come. Anthropogenic climate and broader environmental change only add to the equation; unpredictable weather and increasingly frequent and severe extreme events force people to search for better lives elsewhere – commonly in cities and smaller urban areas. This adds to existing pressures on infrastructure, shelter and employment even as some areas of cities are themselves becoming vulnerable to the effects of climate change. Existing efforts to promote urban sustainability are inadequate and not up to the task of transforming how we build, rebuild, organise and live in cities in the short time still available to achieve this on the basis of the latest worldwide scientific evidence (McPhearson et al, 2016; Simon, 2016; Elmqvist et al, 2018).

The landmark global agreements from 2015 and 2016 – the Sendai Framework for Disaster Risk Reduction, Agenda 2030 and the Sustainable Development Goals (SDGs), the Paris Agreement, and the New Urban Agenda (NUA) – have created new goals and spurred collaborative efforts, emphasising the global responsibilities in 'leaving no one behind', as the United Nations' slogan for the SDGs expresses it (Valencia et al, 2019). Importantly, they represent explicit recognition that achieving more sustainable development cannot be the preserve of national governments but must be pursued at all scales, with 'sub-national entities', that is urban and regional local authorities, playing crucial roles.

Already in 2012, just before the Rio+20 Earth Summit in Rio de Janeiro, the former United Nations (UN) Secretary-General, Ban Ki-moon, declared at a high-level event in

New York that "Our struggle for global sustainability will be won or lost in cities". The diverse urban contexts around the world, therefore, provide a compelling setting for the development of more profound understandings of the processes leading from knowledge to awareness and then to action, individual as well as governmental and societal. This understanding is necessary to be able to improve and increase the 'return' on the massive investments in sustainability and environmental knowledge and evidence-led policy measures. In particular, the SDGs and the NUA have changed the context of research and development, as an increasing number of research funding organisations and research performing organisations are aligning their funding calls and project designs to the SDGs, demanding research projects to contribute directly to the achievement of the goals.

Mistra Urban Futures: a centre for transdisciplinary co-produced research on urban futures

This book provides initial reflections on the innovative agenda of Mistra Urban Futures as it undertakes a coherent programme of international comparative and transdisciplinary co-productive research. The overarching objective of our approach to transdisciplinary comparative research is to analyse how key themes relating to urban sustainability and justice are understood and operationalised in different contexts, thus helping to open up more possibilities for change. The ultimate objective is to ensure the realisation of just and sustainable cities in these different contexts, for example, by learning from both the positive and negative experiences of other cities, and developing trans-local links where knowledge emerges in a common trans-local exploration.

Established in Gothenburg, Sweden, in 2010, Mistra Urban Futures is an international urban research centre ('the Centre' in this book) promoting urban sustainability by means of the transdisciplinary co-production of knowledge, undertaken in a series of Local Interaction Platforms (LIPs). These have been formed through bottom-up local initiatives that lead to formal partnerships among groups of academic and practice-oriented institutions in Gothenburg (Sweden), Sheffield/Greater Manchester (UK), Cape Town (South Africa) and Kisumu (Kenya). These partnerships have come together to form what became Mistra Urban Futures. In 2016–17, a LIP was also established in the Swedish cities of Malmö and Lund in southern Sweden (Skåne Local Interaction Platform) in order to join the Centre, and a smaller partnership in Stockholm is currently in a similar process. The formal nature of all these partnerships is important in terms of their capacity to attract political and financial support, as well as the backing provided to the individual researchers comprising the respective project teams (Mistra Urban Futures, 2015; Palmer and Walasek, 2016; Perry et al, 2018).

These partnerships are diverse in terms of the number of institutional partners, their contractual and governance arrangements, their operating mechanisms, and the types of co-production undertaken. However, all have one or more universities and local authorities as members, thus constituting a particular kind of university–local government partnership (Trencher et al, 2014). All LIP partners share the underlying desire to collaborate on mutually defined applied research priorities in the belief that this offers greater prospects for appropriate and practicable interventions and outcomes than traditional, expert-led research. The Swedish LIPs operate as consortia under multi-year agreements and are hosted by local universities. The Kisumu LIP (KLIP) is constituted as a registered trust under Kenyan law with its own premises, while the Cape Town and Sheffield–Manchester LIPs (CTLIP and SMLIP respectively) are university-based partnerships operating by means of bilateral collaboration agreements with local/regional authority partners (Mistra Urban Futures, 2015; Palmer and Walasek, 2016; Perry et al, 2018).

Mistra Urban Futures is distinctive as a research centre, comprising a Secretariat in Gothenburg and this series of LIP hubs, along with the smaller partnership just established in Stockholm and project-based collaborations in Dehradun and Shimla (India) and Buenos Aires (Argentina). It thus straddles four continents, deliberately embracing the challenges of urban sustainability across the increasingly artificial global North–South divide that still bedevils the UN and many other bi- and multilateral initiatives in an increasingly globalised world of growing diversity at every scale. Core funding is provided by the Swedish Foundation for Strategic Environmental Research (Mistra), the Swedish International Development Cooperation Agency (Sida) and the Gothenburg Consortium of seven partners,[2] which include universities, local and regional authorities and research institutes, with additional local funding in other LIPs and competitive project-based funds from diverse sources.

Until the end of the first five years of the Centre's funding in December 2015, each LIP experimented with its own forms of transdisciplinary knowledge co-production, suited to the particular context and blend of academic and practitioner partners and their respective priorities. Among the most important of these experiences were the breaking down of often longstanding barriers and forging of trust; identification of suitable champions within each institution (ideally at both political and professional levels); development of common approaches to the research; and the role of the LIPs as 'safe spaces' for experimentation away from the constraints and habitual practices of each institution. Considerable effort has been devoted to learning about the experiences using transdisciplinary co-produced research. The Governance and Policy for Sustainability project was an early attempt intended to examine the experiences of the LIPs against a common framework during this first phase.

The LIPs are innovative responses to the challenges of achieving urban sustainability, acting as locally appropriate, safe and experimental convening spaces[3] where the various participating stakeholders can build shared experience and knowledge in the ethos of transdisciplinary co-design, co-creation and co-production. This provides the basis for transcending the confines of their respective institutional parameters, which are now widely acknowledged to be unsuited to tackling the complexities that impede substantive progress towards urban sustainability. Comparative evaluation of the LIP development processes in Cape Town, Kisumu, Manchester and Gothenburg over the period 2010–14 has distilled six necessary conditions for the evolution of LIPs (Perry et al, 2018: 194–5):

- Each platform is anchored between universities and the public sector, with each partner making substantial and meaningful contributions in funding, commitment, in-kind resources, space and active participation.
- Each platform is co-constituted and evolves organically in response to the local context of political and other changes, including election cycles but also major political development such as the devolution processes in both the UK and Kenya.
- All platforms are context-sensitive, aiming at producing not only excellent research but also relevant knowledge, building local credibility and legitimacy. The idea of sustainable urbanisation is shared, but adapted to local issues and challenges.
- Each platform's work is aligned to national and global agendas and also through the nesting of local projects into comparative projects, involving two or more of the local platforms.
- The alignment of local platform work ensures the connection between the platforms and the Centre. This is essential for knowledge to move from local to general insights and for the shared learning processes between the platforms.
- The platform has an important sharing function as a non-aligned and safe place where representatives of stakeholders

share ideas, knowledge, challenges and experiences outside their normal working environs.

This collaborative multi-platform experience has been enhanced and deepened during the period 2016–19, partially by undertaking the comparative research projects explored in this book. On this basis, the multi-stakeholder platform model that operates on the basis of mutual respect and trust, and generates new and often hybrid forms of locally appropriate knowledge and solutions that are simultaneously aligned with national and global agendas, has considerable value in promoting adaptive urban governance more generally.

Mistra Urban Futures has been at the forefront of comparative research on the new global agendas referred to earlier, contributing to the development of the SDGs from the start and participating in the formulation of NUA. In 2014–15, the Centre undertook an extensive pilot study in five cities to test and assess the targets and indicators for the urban goal (SDG 11). The results were used by the UN for the final design of the goals. However, the project also resulted in several articles discussing various aspects of SDG 11 and its implementation in city organisations around the world (see Chapter Six). The Centre has also continued this innovative research by examining co-productively with the respective local authorities how a diverse group of seven cities on four continents are engaging with and implementing the NUA and SDGs. This work forms the subject of Chapter Six.

From local to comparative research

The second phase of Mistra and Sida funding (2016–19) has enabled the negotiation and subsequent introduction of a coherent research framework to guide the research efforts. Entitled Realising Just Cities to reflect the centrality of concerns with urban equity and justice, it comprises three broad themes – socio-spatial, socio-ecological and socio-cultural.

Figure 1.1: Research themes and core processes related to co-production of knowledge

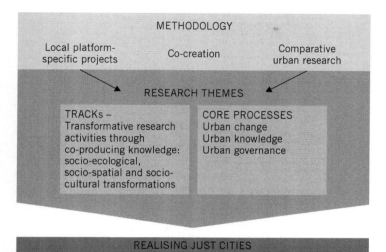

METHODOLOGY

Local platform-specific projects   Co-creation   Comparative urban research

RESEARCH THEMES

TRACKs –
Transformative research
activities through
co-producing knowledge:
socio-ecological,
socio-spatial and socio-
cultural transformations

CORE PROCESSES
Urban change
Urban knowledge
Urban governance

REALISING JUST CITIES

Accessible Green Fair

Source: www.mistraurbanfutures.org

Cross-cutting the themes were three core processes, namely urban change, urban knowledge and urban governance, to provide a mesh of nine subdivisions to ensure that all relevant research interests of the respective LIPs could be catered for in a balanced manner (Figure 1.1). As in the first phase, research projects were identified according to local priorities, but the thematic schema enabled a process of negotiation among LIPs to try to arrive at projects within each theme that were as close as possible in terms of focus as the basis for launching a number of comparative projects, as explained in Chapter Two.

Systematic transdisciplinary comparative research using co-production methods has added a novel and world-leading dimension to Mistra Urban Futures' work. A typology of forms or models of comparison was developed, representing a spectrum in terms of the degree of central versus local (bottom-up)

design, implementation and control (see Chapter Two). Altogether 11 transdisciplinary comparative projects have been initiated to date. All these applied social scientific comparative projects are very different from natural or life science comparative projects, which would require identical and reproducible local projects. As such, they also face distinctive challenges. Because the comparative dimensions of these projects are still at an early stage, our reflections throughout this volume constitute our substantive methodological assessment of what we believe to be the first time that such an exercise has been undertaken, and builds on and upwards from the preliminary assessment published in 2018 (Simon et al, 2018). As such, the principal focus is on the various methods that have emerged within the respective categories of comparison within the typology. Empirical findings are referred to in so far as they are relevant and necessary for a clear understanding of the material, but in the main those findings are being reported in other outputs.

Overview of the book's contents

Despite the project-based chapters being organised around a common set of headings in order to ensure some coherence and comparability in terms of the principal questions and issues that frame the book, they also reveal some diversity of style and balance between empirical and conceptual dimensions. This reflects the nature of the respective projects, their comparative uniformity or local distinctiveness, and the blend of nationalities and professional backgrounds of the author teams. As such, this is a microcosm of the richness in diversity of Mistra Urban Futures and we hope that readers will find it a strength.

Chapter Two explains the evolution of Mistra Urban Futures' research agenda from an almost exclusive focus on research in the individual city platforms during the first phase (2012–15) to a strong emphasis on comparative thematically focused research alongside unilocal projects during the second phase (2016–19).

It presents the typology of possible forms of comparative research identified for this period and the challenges foreseen with the respective categories. The lessons and challenges of managing and tending the research to ensure coherence, along with some wider lessons, are discussed.

In Chapter Three, which addresses solid waste management as a research focus, the concept of retrofitting is applied with a double meaning. It embraces both the challenge of adding a comparative dimension with Helsingborg to the initial local project in Kisumu, and the challenge of retrofitting new waste management strategies on to the inadequacies and piecemeal nature of waste collection and management in the latter city. Despite the sharply different prevailing conditions in the two cities, there has been a strong emphasis on bidirectional learning, including how appropriate solutions in Kisumu might hold valuable lessons for Malmö, which has experienced a technological lock-in to waste incineration for many years.

Replication of local projects across cities constitutes the subject of Chapter Four, which is based on three comparative projects on knowledge exchange, food and transport respectively. These have been undertaken in and between Cape Town, Kisumu and Gothenburg, and, in one case, also Malmö. The replication challenges are addressed in relation to three sets of issues, namely quantitative research, qualitative research and the context-specific social development interventions. The extent of diversity required that the main replicative comparison took place at the level of broad objectives, with attention to underlying values, rather than detailed methods or empirical evidence.

Chapter Five differs markedly from the others in that it documents carefully and reflects on the extensive and thoughtfully reflective process of project planning and development just taking place for new work on urban development and migration. Themed around the intention to build clusters and assemblages, it has engaged researchers in Gothenburg, Malmö and Kisumu.

Chapter Six reports on the highly distinctive project studying the extent to which seven of the eight cities where Mistra Urban Futures works on four continents are engaging with and implementing the NUA and urban SDG. It is the only example of the project category that is centrally designed – necessitated by the global agendas that form the subject matter. Nevertheless, it is being implemented in different ways according to local circumstances in each city. The clear narrative also reflects the high degree of integration achieved among team members.

Chapter Seven provides another distinctive perspective on the work done by Mistra Urban Futures, by reflecting on how one particular form of transdisciplinary learning has taken place within the SMLIP. This is not the co-production of new knowledge through research, although the activity concerned was undertaken as part of a comparative learning project. Instead, the chapter explores another form of meaningful participation and transdisciplinary learning that took place through an exchange and reflection on perceptions about a specific event among local authority officials, citizen/civil society researchers and academics, in order to formulate a shared understanding of the most useful learnings for Greater Manchester.

Finally, Chapter Eight provides a synthesis and draws conclusions from the rest of the book, reflecting the overall conceptual framings of the suite of comparative projects and the diversity as expressed through the successive chapters. It also reflects on the ways in which this innovative research programme has advanced the achievement of just and sustainable cities, as well as advancing the field of transdisciplinary co-production, for which there is rapidly increasing demand.

Notes

[1] Robert Chambers has been a lifelong pioneer and exponent of participatory methodologies, and his most recent book (Chambers, 2017), which contextualises his cumulative reflections, provides a succinct overview.

[2] University of Gothenburg, Chalmers University of Technology, IVL Swedish Environmental Research Institute, City of Gothenburg, County Administrative Board of Western Sweden, Region Västra Götaland, the Gothenburg Region (GR).

[3] These are also sometimes referred to as boundary or boundary-crossing spaces, functions or organisations.

References

Brandsen, T. and Honingh, M. (2016) 'Distinguishing different types of co-production: a conceptual analysis based on the classical definitions', *Public Administration Review*, 76(3): 427–35. doi: 10.1111/puar.12465

Cabannes, Y. (2004) 'Participatory budgeting: a significant contribution to participatory democracy', *Environment & Urbanization*, 16(1): 27–46. doi: 10.1177/095624780401600104

Cabannes, Y. (2015) 'The impact of participatory budgeting on basic services: municipal practices and evidence from the field', *Environment & Urbanization*, 27(1): 257–84. doi: 10.1177/0956247815572297

Chambers, R. (2017) *Can We Know Better? Reflections for Development*, Rugby: Practical Action Publishing.

Dempsey, N., Bramley, G., Power, S. and Brown, C. (2011) 'The social dimension of sustainable development: defining urban social sustainability', *Sustainable Development*, 19(5): 289–300. doi: 10.1002/sd.417

Durose, C. and Richardson, L. (eds) (2016) *Designing Public Policy for Co-Production: Theory, Practice and Change*, Bristol: Policy Press.

Durose, C., Richardson, L. and Perry, B. (2018) 'Craft metrics to value co-production', *Nature*, 562: 32–3. doi: 10.1038/d41586-018-06860-w

Elmqvist, T., Bai, X., Frantzeskaki, N., Griffith, C., Maddox, D., McPhearson, T., Parnell, S., Romero-Lankao, P., Simon, D. and Watkins, M. (eds) *Urban Planet*, Cambridge: Cambridge University Press. Available from: www.cambridge.org/9781107196933

Jasanoff, S. (2004) 'The idiom of co-production', in S. Jasanoff (ed) *States of Knowledge: The Co-Production of Science and Social Order*, London: Routledge, pp 1–12.

Joshi, A. and Moore, M. (2004), 'Institutionalised co-production: unorthodox public service delivery in challenging environments', *Journal of Development Studies*, 40(1): 31–49. doi: 10.1080/00220380410001673184

Mauser, W., Klepper, G., Rice, M., Schmalzbauer, B.S., Hackmann, H., Leemans, R. and Moore, H. (2013) 'Transdisciplinary global change research: the co-creation of knowledge for sustainability', *Current Opinion in Environmental Sustainability*, 5(3–4): 420–31. doi: 10.1016/j.cosust.2013.07.001

McPhearson, T., Parnell, S., Simon, D., Gaffney, O., Elmqvist, T., Bai, X., Roberts, D. and Revi, A. (2016) 'Scientists must have a say in the future of cities' (comment), *Nature*, 538: 165–7.

Mistra Urban Futures (2015) *Strategic Plan 2016–19 Revised 16 November 2015*, Gothenburg: Mistra Urban Futures.

Mitlin, D. (2008) 'With and beyond the state – co-production as a route to political influence, power and transformation for grassroots organizations', *Environment & Urbanization*, 20(2): 339–60. doi: 10.1177/0956247808096117

Palmer, H. and Walasek, H. (eds) (2016) *Co-production in Action*, Gothenburg: Mistra Urban Futures. Available from: www.mistraurbanfutures.org/en/annual-conference/conference-book

Parks, R.B., Baker, P.C., Kiser, L., Oakerson, R., Ostrom, E., Ostrom, V., Percy, S.L., Vandivort, M.B., Whitaker, G.P. and Wilson, R. (1981) 'Consumers as co-producers of public services: some economic and institutional considerations', *Policy Studies Journal*, 9(7): 1001–11. doi: 10.1111/j.1541-0072.1981.tb01208.x

Perry, B., Patel, Z., Norén Bretzer, Y. and Polk, M. (2018) 'Organising for co-production: local interaction platforms for urban sustainability', *Politics and Governance*, 6(1): 189–98. doi: 10.17645/pag.v6i1.1228

Polk, M. (ed) (2015a) *Co-Producing Knowledge for Sustainable Cities: Joining Forces for Change*, Abingdon and New York, NY: Routledge.

Polk, M. (2015b) 'Transdisciplinary co-production: designing and testing a transdisciplinary research framework for societal problem solving', *Futures*, 65: 110–22. doi: 10.1016/j.futures.2014.11.001

Schaer, C. and Komlavi Hanonou, E. (2017) 'The real governance of disaster risk management in peri-urban Senegal: delivering flood response services through co-production', *Progress in Development Studies*, 17(1): 38–53. doi: 10.1177/1464993416674301

Simon, D. (ed.) (2016) *Rethinking Sustainable Cities: Accessible, Green and Fair*, Bristol: Policy Press.

Simon, D., Palmer, H., Smit, W., Riise, J. and Valencia, S. (2018) 'The challenges of transdisciplinary co-production: from unilocal to comparative research', *Environment & Urbanization*, 30(2): 481–500. doi: 10.1177/0956247818787177. Available from: http://journals.sagepub.com/doi/full/10.1177/0956247818787177

Trencher, G., Bai, X., Evans, J., McCormick, K. and Yarime, M. (2014) 'University partnerships for co-designing and co-producing urban sustainability', *Global Environmental Change*, 28: 153–65. doi: 10.1016/j.gloenvcha.2014.06.009

Valencia, S.C., Simon, D., Croese, S., Nordqvist, J., Oloko, M., Sharma, T., Taylor Buck, N. and Versace, I. (2019) 'Adapting the Sustainable Development Goals and the New Urban Agenda to the city level: initial reflections from a comparative research project', *International Journal of Urban Sustainable Development*, 11(1): 4–23. doi: 10.1080/19463138.2019.1573172

Wolf, G. and Mahaffey, N. (2016) 'Designing difference: co-production of spaces of potentiality', *Urban Planning*, 1(1): 59–67. doi: 10.17645/up.v1i1.540

TWO

From unilocal to comparative research: the Mistra Urban Futures journey

Henrietta Palmer and David Simon

Introduction

In terms of the logic laid out in Chapter One, this chapter moves from the locally co-produced transdisciplinary research in individual city platforms to the even more experimental approach of comparing such local research approaches across varying urban contexts.

Understanding the potential uniqueness of cities and the specificity of the local are essential for knowledge production for sustainability. Local practices stemming from a specific climate and ecology, a specific geographic setting and urban morphology, a set of cultures and traditions, and local social networks, skills and habits interact with national and global agendas to produce different and contextualised solutions from which to learn also about universal problems. This implies that urban dissimilarity and difference are interesting features for research on urban sustainability that could potentially be captured through comparison. The organisational structure of Mistra Urban Futures, as presented in Chapter One, carefully considers the differences among the partnering platforms in terms of local stakeholder participation and agreements. Nevertheless, the raison d'être for this organisational structure calls for comparison between the different cities and their respective stakeholder arrangements. Comparison is embodied in the notion of the Centre as it spans different kinds of borders at global, continental and national scales. Consequently, comparison is a constant ongoing process in which each issue is positioned and debated. To pursue comparative research across the different LIPs, to produce further knowledge on sustainable development, was therefore an underlying aspiration that found expression in the structured propositions embodied in the Centre's Strategic Plan 2016–19 (Mistra Urban Futures, 2015).

Collaborative comparative research is not novel and further diversifies urban comparison as it bridges different urban contexts and research agencies into the varying contexts (Gough, 2012). However, as with unilocally co-designed and produced research, comparative research does not avoid the importance of understanding and engaging with the implicit and explicit power relations. Who will decide what to compare in such a multi-collaborative setup? After all, what is of apparent value to one context and to its multi-stakeholder structure might lack relevance and/or interest from the other comparative contexts. For Mistra Urban Futures, the jointly developed research agenda of Realising Just Cities – introduced in the previous chapter – has been a useful framework for selecting possible comparative themes from a common rationale. Here we examine the substantive themes that were considered relevant for comparative investigation into the larger issue of 'prospects for the just city' (Clarke, 2010: 9).

Comparative urban research has been oscillating in popularity over several decades, even having a dedicated international academic journal in the 1970s and 1980s,[1] a key focus of which was the global South. Early theoretical challenges and formulations were also debated in urban and some disciplinary journals, particularly in relation to problems of decolonisation and post-colonial urbanism (for example Walton, 1975; Abu-Lughod, 1975; Simon, 1984, 1989, 1992; King, 1990). More recent theoretical approaches have also been applied in this arena (such as Roy, 2011, 2016). At one point, some comparative research focusing on identifying networks of world cities was heavily criticised as performing hierarchical division of cities in terms of which cities are of value to compare with and which ones are not (Robinson, 2011). Pointing towards this embedded power mechanism of comparative urban research, Jennifer Robinson underlined the importance not only of a broad inclusion of cities but also of exploratory methodologies in comparison. To compare case studies of good solutions or non-functioning solutions might be less relevant for 'cities in a world of cities' connected through different kinds of processes and movements. She therefore calls for 'new repertoires of comparativism' to expand its potentials beyond the global North–South divide and beyond any normative definition and division of cities of the world and to be potentially " 'generative", where variation across shared features provides a basis for generating conceptual insights supported by the multiple, sometimes interconnected, theoretical conversations which enable global urban studies' (Robinson, 2016: 195).

In the work reported here, we contribute to this new repertoire. This research programme is both a substantive contribution to the discourse on urban justice through comparative and sometimes conceptual inquiry, and a methodological contribution showing how co-produced transdisciplinary research can cater for some of the main issues discussed within comparative urban research, such as negotiation and contestation of the research issues, differences of cultures theory, and translation of knowledge (McFarlane, 2010). Co-produced transdisciplinary comparative research sets out a new dimension of including participants from sectors beyond academia. Jane M. Jacobs identifies a reason for doing collaborative research comparatively, which resonates with the ethos of

Mistra Urban Futures' research approach, namely that the kind of 'comparisons that city builders, managers, transnational workers, and residents engage in – is essential for redrawing the map of urban studies. In this sense, urban practitioners may be ahead of urban theorists' (Jacobs, 2012: 920). Further, our comparative work is organised according to a defined typological framework, which will be explained later in this chapter and in depth in the chapters to follow. Both there and in the concluding chapter, we assess the extent to which the typology is valuable or generative.

The remainder of this chapter is divided into four sections. The next section provides an overview of methodological lessons derived from the first phase of Mistra Urban Futures' research, in which transdisciplinary co-produced studies were undertaken locally within the individual cities. The third section discusses the reasons for doing comparative co-produced research and the challenges involved in doing this research transition. The fourth section proposes a framework for comparative co-production. The final section provides a concluding discussion and a description of the chapter's contributions. Parts of this chapter draw heavily on earlier published work on this comparative research agenda (Simon et al, 2018).

Methodological lessons from unilocal transdisciplinary co-produced research

This section synthesises some of the key achievements, constraints and generalisable methodological principles based on the experience in the respective LIPs during the first phase of Mistra Urban Futures. It draws in part on the work of Henrietta Palmer and Helen Walasek (2016) and Beth Perry and colleagues (2018).

As emphasised in Chapter One, key features of the LIPs are their diverse histories, structures, number, and range of partner institutions and activities. The first important lesson reflects that the prerequisite for success is being locally appropriate and embedded, so as to be, and be seen to be, responsive to local conditions and flexible in adapting to evolving agendas. Attempting to establish a common format for LIPs to undertake transdisciplinary research co-production in different contexts would simply not work and therefore the starting point for comparison is the acknowledgement of difference rather than similarity.

In spite of their differences, the LIPs operate in a similar manner as 'active intermediaries', a term introduced by Beth Perry and Tim May (2010) for governance structures acting between global agendas and local contexts and concerns, translating and transforming practices of knowledge production among the different partners involved. As a second lesson, this tells how this bidirectional role and relationship add considerable value both ways. On the one hand, the individual cities have been able to understand and learn from experiences elsewhere and from global initiatives on urban sustainability in tackling similar problems. Conversely, Mistra Urban Futures uses the transdisciplinary co-production experiences in the individual cities to inform wider global policy debates and agendas for practice.

A third learning is that the partners need to operate through thorough reflexivity, with openness to change and renewal (May and Perry, 2011, 2018; Voss and Bornemann, 2011). A perennial challenge in any large institution, but one that is magnified in transdisciplinary partnerships, is the difficulty of maintaining continuity, consistency and momentum in the face of ongoing changes in key personnel in one or more partners. A change in mayor, chief executive, or even line manager of a particular institutional representative can change priorities, power relations within and across partner institutions, political and/or financial support, or even enthusiasm to participate. New team members often raise new questions (or repeat old ones) and may challenge previous decisions or have different priorities, and the renegotiations involved can be draining, even when there is agreement in principle to abide by previous decisions (see also discussions in subsequent chapters).

Another important lesson is that much depends on who the individual researchers are. It is essential to identify researchers who can have a pronounced interest in straddling disciplines and bridging the divide between academia and policy/practice, since these are extremely difficult and time-consuming challenges and not everybody has the right personality, skills, experience or such career ambitions. A related acquired knowledge is that different stakeholders often have diverse perspectives and conflicting agendas. People involved in transdisciplinary research also need good facilitation skills or need to be able to draw on professional facilitators, as they attempt to reconcile or make room for diverging perspectives in both process and outcomes (Pohl et al, 2010).

Experience from each LIP shows that it is possible to have a significant impact on policy and practice through the transdisciplinary co-production of knowledge. For example, co-production processes that brought together different stakeholders in Kisumu resulted in the planning of a range of physical upgrading projects for the city and the implementation of a number of significant initiatives, such as an eco-tourism project. Several processes have also brought together officials and researchers to co-produce new policies, such as a new policy framework to guide state investment in human settlements in the Western Cape (the location of Cape Town) and a new climate change strategy for Gothenburg. Exposing both the participating academics and practitioners to a range of new perspectives from different cultures of knowledges and contextual experience has triggered the creation of new communities of knowledge and practice with capacity to change the mindsets and actions of many participants (Palmer and Walasek, 2016).

A final key lesson is that there is no single, right method of approaching the transdisciplinary co-production of knowledge, and this kind of research usually needs many different methods depending of the stage of the research process where the intentions and short-term objectives might vary, but also on who is participating; how contested that particular issue is; what the existing body of knowledge on that particular topic is in that particular place; and how experienced the participants are in doing co-produced transdisciplinary research. One commonality in the various transdisciplinary co-production processes taking place was that they all involved extensive engagement over a sustained period of time, including a range of stakeholders to attempt to better understand and address the real challenges facing the city.

A transition towards comparative transdisciplinary co-production: challenges foreseen

This section provides arguments for the objectives of comparing co-produced transdisciplinary research in an urban context. It presents the sub-projects of this comparative research, and discusses some assumed outcomes in relation to potential impact.

Reasons for comparing co-produced and transdisciplinary research

After the end of Phase 1 (2012–15) of Mistra's funding, the Centre sharpened its focus on how to transition towards sustainable cities by suggesting comparative transdisciplinary research as a possible approach to tackle 'wicked' problems[2] of urban injustice. With the diverse experiences from the four city platforms, where at that point the different stakeholders involved in the respective LIPs were already experienced in co-production, there was also good potential to move forward with comparative research on what constitutes a just city and how to realise such a city in contrasting urban contexts.

Sustainable development is a contested term, and conflicts can appear in determining what constitutes a socially, economically and ecologically desirable urban condition. The question of 'sustainable development for whom?' emerges sooner or later. For all the research conducted within the different platforms, urban justice was already an embedded objective. Within the three broad themes of socio-spatial, socio-ecological and socio-cultural transformations, three core attributes were considered to characterise just and sustainable cities, according to the Mistra Urban Futures vision statement (2015: 9) – that they should be fair, green and accessible. Since comparative transdisciplinary co-produced research had the potential to catalyse new knowledge about certain themes as well as around what Jacobs calls the 'third term' (2012), in other words the meta-issue evolving through thinking across different cases, it was relevant to move a step further to explore the realisation of urban justice through a 'comparative gaze' to extend the Centre's co-produced research.

Existing comparative urban concepts such as twinning have already created comparative exchanges between the city officials for mutual learning about, for example, planning mechanisms. City branding listings, where urban qualities such as liveability are measured to compete for the same group of investors, represent another form of comparison with which the public and private stakeholders were familiar. However, this kind of comparative urban studies were new to the participants from the public and private sectors. Also, from an academic perspective, the co-produced comparative approach was at large untried and came with certain difficulties to imagine. However, the new wave of theoretically inspired comparative urban studies, mentioned in the introduction, calls for a fresh view on comparison where cities are not comparatively graded but linked and connected both conceptually and by different kinds of global processes, and hence could be compared according to various differing logics. Robinson (2016) presents a taxonomy of possible types and features of urban comparisons: from light touch 'comparative gestures' to comparisons of tracing connections, and of launching analysis and generating concept from specific contexts with possible wider applications. Mistra Urban Futures' approach of co-produced transdisciplinary comparisons could speak to many of these types, but also adds yet another layer of methodology to the development of the discourse. All these anchor points, together with the positioning of experimental comparative urbanism as part of the evolving field of post-colonial urbanism, added compelling features to the prospect, which mitigated anticipated complexities and difficulties.

Indeed, comparing transnationally how to realise just cities implies an agenda that cannot 'belong' to the interest of any particular stakeholder group or practice, nor to one single geographical context. All perspectives, conflicting as well as aligned, ultimately contribute to the production of a richer body of knowledge on what urban justice could look like, and how it might be imagined, operationalised and achieved. Since each one of the individual comparative projects came to formulate its own rationale for comparison, Mistra Urban Futures set up an overall comparative project, entitled Realising Just Cities. This comparative endeavour aimed to produce meta-knowledge, considering how all the different comparative sub-projects together create societal impact in terms of organisational changes and policy effects, along with changed social behaviours and societal imaginaries and visions, all contributing to the realisation of just cities.[3]

Learning from comparative co-produced research

As has been pointed out elsewhere within the work of Mistra Urban Futures, different organisational setups contribute to different kinds of knowledge production. Consequently, as part of a comparative learning process, the differing organisational project arrangements could also be compared, along with the different co-production methods applied at similar stages of the respective processes in the varying contexts. Both these objectives would feed into the cross-context learning on how to achieve just cities. Hierarchies that might exist in one context, and that could effectively prohibit deliberative co-production, might be understood in light of shared experiences from other situations, where structures of power would take different forms. In this manner, the methods and organisational structures applied could develop and become more robust. This, in turn, would contribute further insights into transdisciplinary knowledge production and more sustainable processes of co-production.

Another objective underlying the comparative co-produced research is to mirror the way different problems are manifested in their respective local contexts, in order to deepen our understanding of the problem at hand and its global impact and relevance. Highlighting differences or similarities, or embracing a diversity of knowledge cultures, allows for an expanded understanding of the problem – something a single context could not produce. In other situations, a crucial problem might be suppressed and hence become 'non-existent' within an agenda promoting urban justice, as for example is embraced in the discourse on recognition (Fraser, 1996). Transnational comparative and co-produced research, with its multitude of stakeholders, could shed light on and highlight such an issue. A striking example is the way the #MeToo movement, addressing the matter of silenced sexual abuse, has been brought forward as a parallel discourse in diverse contexts around the world through experiential knowledge and an international co-acknowledgement.

In Mistra Urban Futures' comparative proposal, 11 thematically different projects were identified, resulting from the previous three broad themes of socio-spatial, socio-ecological and socio-cultural transformations, covering an urban ground of great variety – from food production to migration (see Table 2.1). While using these different topic lenses to understand how urban justice might be achieved, a further outcome would be to detect the direction and intensity of ongoing change in each local context. How change is taking place, and how it could be directed towards more just urban conditions through different vehicles of transformation, could be explored at a comparative meta-level traceable across the full set of projects. Here each context would provide valuable insights on mechanisms for transformation towards urban justice, and how they play out in relation to different citizen groups.

Unlike 'traditional' research, co-produced research has the advantage of already including some of the actors with planning roles or mandates (such as city officials and councillors). This means that the research, in addition to pointing to evidence and results, actually becomes a catalyst itself, affecting behavioural changes as part of the research process. The novelty of our methodological approach is not collaboration per se within a research team, but to have multiple research teams of different stakeholders, each one with local expertise, in a joint comparison. With different local stakeholders engaged in the comparative issue, conversations are generated from stakeholder to stakeholder across geographical contexts. In the process, the comparative issue becomes nested in a number of cross-national conversations that, however difficult to foresee, would undoubtedly affect each local environment. We return to a discussion around these matters in the concluding chapter of this book, detecting the impact of our work.

Early assumed outcomes

Clearly, outcomes and impacts are, and will be, difficult to specify in this ambitious programme, although it is coming towards its end in terms of financing. Many of the project setups are at this point concerned with academic outputs, network effects and different outcomes in terms of learning and sharing. However, this in itself is worth commenting on, since outputs such as constructed networks and outcomes such as shared knowledge point towards an expansion of a culture dealing with joint explorative and problem-solving research, which in itself is a transformative tool for societal change. The researchers and practitioners involved foresee an extended research activity, beyond their immediate research engagements or their daily managements, that will enable a joint space for translation of concepts and cultures. The comparative issue is in many situations envisioned as an 'arena' into which different stakeholders are invited to test new thinking and where new knowledge could be produced. The LIPs have proved before to provide 'safe spaces' for untraditional research practices (Perry et al, 2018). Ultimately this exploration and production of knowledge will broaden the bases for decisions and for policies and new research to follow.

A typological framework for comparative transdisciplinary knowledge co-production

In this section, we present the framework developed as a methodological support for the comparative imagination within Mistra Urban Futures. We further present and discuss briefly how the substantive sub-themes relate to the typologies and the overall research objective of Realising Just Cities.

According to Colin McFarlane (2010), empirical urban comparative studies are mostly concerned with the practicalities of the research, the methodology or the categories. As we have described, co-produced transdisciplinary comparative research involves numerous practicalities in terms of logistics and finance as well as in terms of setting principles and agreements for research and about the research findings. This research approach can make use of a number of methodologies in relation to the participants, the particular stage of the research process and the need for either short or long research objectives. In a multidimensional project of this kind, conducted both as an overarching and Centre-initiated proposal, as well as thematically organised comparative transnational projects, additionally containing several local multi-stakeholder research groups, some overarching directions are crucial. Typologies as a framework for comparison have in our case been a helpful instrument to set the stage and to create a common cognition from which to thread forward in varying directions.

As the Centre developed its research towards the Realising Just Cites research agenda, a typology of six possible categories of how comparative transdisciplinary knowledge co-production could take place was developed collectively by the LIP directors and Secretariat. This framework informed the Strategic Plan 2016–20, thus preceding initiation of the research. It functioned both descriptively to formulate for external stakeholders what the Centre was about to undertake, and productively to guide everyone involved across all the platforms in terms of the comparative ethos. The following categories were conceptualised:

- *local projects retrofitted*, where existing research projects on a particular theme in different cities were in need of some retrofitting, or perhaps just a specific comparative 'add-on', to facilitate drawing conclusions about that particular theme from multiple contexts;
- *local projects replicated*, where particular successful projects initiated in particular cities have been, or are intended to be, replicated in other cities, thus opening up possibilities for cross-city comparison of problems and solutions;
- *translocally clustered comparative research projects*, developing consistent clusters of projects identified by a common theme rather than immediate comparative features, across multiple cities to produce new references for urban research and practice;
- *internationally initiated projects with local co-production*, internationally conceived through co-design, with co-production undertaken by local teams in each city, but with centrally based co-ordination;
- *international projects with translocal co-production*, where completely translocal teams work across cities;
- *PhD studentships linked to co-production processes*, where either students from one city are doing research on another city

in collaboration with local students, or students are doing comparative research on a number of cities. This model is distinct from types 1–5 in that, as the projects are led by PhD students, it also includes an educational element.

This typology provided a spectrum of central versus diverse local design and implementation, and helped us set out a direction for the comparative projects in addition to the Realising Just Cities research agenda. It was resolved at the outset not to be prescriptive or proscriptive. So, examples of several models were expected to emerge according to the nature of the initial impetus in each case, the subject matter and degree of diversity or uniformity in relevant local projects, and the number of platforms participating in each theme.

The foci for the comparative research projects emerged from an iterative process of negotiation among the LIPs and Centre Secretariat based on relevance and interests for the LIPs in the suggested sub-themes. This negotiation sought to ensure overall coverage of the three broad themes into which the Realising Just Cities research agenda had been divided (socio-spatial, socio-ecological and socio-cultural transformations), along with cross-cutting core processes of urban change, urban knowledge and urban governance (see Figure 1.1). The large variation of possible sub-themes together with the six comparative categories in the typology would guarantee a broad spectrum of findings that jointly would produce relevant and possibly new knowledge on how to realise just cities, as well as bring new concepts and innovative methods to the discourse on comparative urbanism.

The initial expectation of a diversity of comparative models has been borne out, in that examples of all except the fifth category have been pursued. The exception, framed as a centrally initiated project with translocal co-production, turned out to be unfeasible given budgetary and capacity limitations, as everybody in such a project team would need to spend a

Table 2.1: Mistra Urban Futures' comparative projects

Project	Platforms
Realising Just Cities	All
Cultural Heritage and Just Cities	CTLIP, GOLIP, KLIP, SMLIP
Food Value Chain	CTLIP, GOLIP, KLIP, SMLIP
Implementing the New Urban Agenda and the SDGs	All
Knowledge Exchange	CTLIP, SKLIP
Migration and Urban Development	GOLIP, KLIP, SKLIP
Neighbourhood Transformation and Housing Justice	GOLIP, SMLIP
Participatory Cities	All
Solid Waste Management	KLIP, SKLIP
Transport and Sustainable Urban Development	CTLIP, GOLIP, KLIP
Urban Public Finance	CTLIP, KLIP

significant amount of time in each city involved. Not only would this be prohibitively costly, but most researchers and partners from outside academia would have difficulty in obtaining leave of absence for the periods required. In the light of climate change, moreover, the degree of travel required for this kind of research must also be questioned.

Two of the 11 comparative projects (Table 2.1) have been adopted by consensus as universal, in which all LIPs are participating, representing different comparative categories. The more advanced project initially was a centrally designed but locally adapted and implemented project on how the involved cities engage with and implement (or not) the United Nations Human Settlements Programme's New Urban Agenda (NUA) and the Sustainable Development Goals (SDGs), especially the urban SDG (SDG 11). This project also involved two specific project-based partnerships in Shimla (India) and Buenos Aires (Argentina). The second universal project, entitled Realising Just Cities (deliberately echoing the name of the general research framework), was framed as a reflective research by each LIP team regarding how its diverse activities and projects are advancing Mistra Urban Futures' core objectives of urban sustainability and justice. As such, it represented a project of meta-learning rather than a specific comparative project type, and as it developed it left the comparative project portfolio and took on the role of a formative evaluation of the comprehensive research achievement responding to the Centre's mission 'to generate and use knowledge for transitions towards sustainable urban futures through reflective co-creation at local and global levels' (Mistra Urban Futures, 2015: 9).

The other nine comparative project themes were defined as Food Value Chain; Solid Waste Management; Cultural Heritage and Just Cities; Participatory Cities; Migration and Urban Development; Transport and Sustainable Urban Development; Neighbourhood Transformation and Housing Justice; Urban Public Finance; and Knowledge Exchange.

Each comparative project has different origins and rationales, and different numbers of participating LIPs. For instance, the comparative food research has grown out of several foregoing comparative food projects involving the African Centre for Cities/Cape Town LIP and Kisumu LIP, including Consuming Urban Poverty and the Hungry Cities Partnership, so considerable comparative quantitative and qualitative research work had already been undertaken in those projects. The focus was now broadened somewhat to accommodate other LIPs, particularly in Gothenburg and Sheffield–Manchester, where interests focus on allotment cultivation and augmentation of urban food supply; urban commoning; active engagement of refugees with agricultural skills and the need to earn livelihoods; and the reduction of food miles. This broad focus on food justice represents a replicated comparative project, along with research on solid waste management and comparative work on how knowledge transfers from public sectors to academia and vice versa. Public finance is at the other end of the scale, the smallest comparative project, having grown out of a PhD project comparing the municipal financial systems in the cities of Cape Town and Kisumu.

The category based on transnational PhD collaboration has its very successful forerunner in a model set up with special funding from the Swedish International Development Cooperation Agency as a mutual learning process between PhD students at the Gothenburg and Kisumu platforms. The four Swedish and three Kenyan PhD students, together with their supervisors, co-developed an innovative but complex learning and research process. This had both cross-national co-production as a basis for some of the PhD projects, and cross-national comparison and learning among the PhDs themselves, in the form of common seminars, courses and exchanges. Besides the development of the seven theses, the participants and tutors have also been developing reflexive work on the process itself (Jernsand and Kraff, 2016). However, when the new comparative work was launched in 2016, the PhD category was ultimately omitted, due to the lack of funding for new PhD positions.

Taken together, these projects and their respective themes represent a good amalgam of the respective platforms' particular local priorities and broad coverage of the Realising Just Cities agenda. Reassuringly, they also correspond well to topical comparative research themes identified in the literature, where urban politics on sustainability, urban justice, the cultural turn in urban studies, and mobility and migration as well as methodological and theoretical advances in comparative urban research are highlighted (Clarke, 2010; Robinson, 2011, 2016; Roy, 2011, 2016; Glick Schiller, 2012; Gough, 2012; Jacobs, 2012; Simon, 2015).

Discussion

This final section comments on some main features of the proposed methodology and typologies in relation to the chapters to follow.

As a multidimensional research approach set out from the base of a Centre organised around multiple city platforms, the comparative agenda set out here is indeed challenging and risky. The explicit challenges from each sub-project will become apparent in the following chapters. The close interconnections between process and outcomes in this kind of research, and how the construction of a research process also affects the research objectives, will also be visualised. McFarlane (2010) tells us that efforts to learn between cultures of theory raise ethical and political considerations. In transdisciplinary co-production, these are already pressing but acknowledged matters, as the knowledge cultures involved are varied and have to find room for both conflicts and negotiations in processes of knowledge integration. Nevertheless, it brings us to constantly consider which knowledge counts and who sets the pre-conditions for the knowledge production. In our case, the project emerged from local concerns that had been the bases for co-produced local investigations and, when seen through a larger framework of Realising Just Cities, would start to build relations across platforms and across multi-stakeholder research groups. Relevance to local context is crucial, and as the complexity of the large proposal also makes it vulnerable, it will not find its driving motivation if it does not resonate with the local actors involved.

As explained at the end of Chapter One, the following chapters are each presented as a larger 'case' (sometimes consisting of more than one thematic research project), debating the relevance of the typologies foreseen and how reflecting on these have contributed to the process of the research. Thus Chapter Three discusses retrofitting as a comparative strategy in a study of waste management. Chapter Four reflects on replicating as a comparative approach between three different research teams concerned with an educational knowledge exchange programme set in place at two different LIPs: food security, and transportation and urban development. Chapter Five reflects how clustering has been a helpful typology through which to organise and analyse a number of discrete projects on migration and urban development. Chapter Six discusses strategies for building a centrally organised comparative project with multiple local teams in relation to the implementation of SDG 11 and the NUA. Chapter Seven showcases a local collaborative project that explores the relevance for comparative work of transdisciplinary learning within a team comprising academics, local authority officers and non–governmental organisation staff. The final chapter provides a concluding discussion and reflection of this agenda and its potential for adaptation, together with a discussion on potential contribution of the comparative work to the Centre's agenda of Realising Just Cities.

Notes

[1] *Comparative Urban Research* was edited by William John Hanna and published by Transaction Periodicals Consortium at Rutgers University, New Jersey, USA, but ceased publication due to declining interest and support.

[2] 'Wicked' problems are those complex, hard-to-define problems that do not lend themselves to single, permanent or replicable solutions (Rittel and Webber, 1973).

[3] Realising Just Cities is the title of both the framework explained in Chapter One and of a comparative project. The latter includes comparative inquiries at each LIP, examining the platform's role as active intermediaries and the importance of reflexivity in seeking to detect so-called second- and third-order effects. It includes further components than the ten comparative projects only, hence its full structural framework is not entirely relevant to describe in this context of comparative project methodology.

References

Abu-Lughod, J. (1975) 'The legitimacy of comparisons in comparative urban studies: a theoretical position and an application to North African cities', *Urban Affairs Review*, 11(1): 13–35. doi: 10.1177/107808747501100102

Clarke, S.E. (2010) 'Emerging research agendas in comparative urban research', Paper presented to the Political Studies Association Annual Conference, Edinburgh. Available from: www.researchgate. net/profile/Susan_Clarke10/publication/228377415_Emerging_ Research_Agendas_in_Comparative_Urban_Research/links/ 55628e0108ae86c06b65f46c/Emerging-Research-Agendas-in-Comparative-Urban-Research.pdf

Fraser, N. (1996) 'Social justice in the age of identity politics: redistribution, recognition and participation', Tanner Lectures on Human Values, Stanford University, 30 April – 2 May.

Glick Schiller, N. (2012) 'A comparative relative perspective on the relationships between migrants and cities', *Urban Geography*, 33(6): 879–903. doi: 10.2747/0272-3638.33.6.879

Gough, K.V. (2012) 'Reflections on conducting urban comparison', *Urban Geography*, 33(6): 866–878. doi: 10.2747/0272-3638.33.6.866

Jacobs, J.M. (2012) 'Commentary: comparing comparative urbanisms', *Urban Geography*, 33(6): 904–14. doi: 10.2747/0272-3638.33.6.904

Jernsand, E. M. and Kraff, H. (2016) 'Collaborative PhDs: new approaches, challenges and opportunities', in H. Palmer and H. Walasek (eds) *Co-Production in Action*, Gothenburg: Mistra Urban Futures, pp 76–83. Available from: www.mistraurbanfutures.org/ en/annual-conference/conference-book

King, A.D. (1990) *Urbanism, Colonialism and the World-Economy: Cultural and Spatial Foundations of the World Urban System*, London and New York, NY: Routledge.

May, T. and Perry, B. (2011) 'A way forward: active intermediaries', in T May and B Perry (eds), *Social Research and Reflexivity: Content, Consequence and Context*, London: Sage.

May, T. and Perry, B. (2018) *Reflexivity: The Essential Guide*, London: Sage.

McFarlane, C. (2010) 'The comparative city: knowledge, learning, urbanism', *International Journal of Urban and Regional Research*, 34(4): 725–42. doi: 10.1111/j.1468-2427.2010.00917.x

Mistra Urban Futures (2015) *Strategic Plan 2016–2019*, Gothenburg: Mistra Urban Futures. Available from: www.mistraurbanfutures. org/sites/mistraurbanfutures.org/files/strategicplan-rev-final-20nov2015.pdf

Palmer, H. and Walasek, H. (eds) (2016) *Co-Production in Action*, Gothenburg: Mistra Urban Futures. Available from: www. mistraurbanfutures.org/en/annual-conference/conference-book

Perry, B. and May, T. (2010) 'Urban knowledge exchange: devilish dichotomies and active intermediation', *International Journal of Knowledge-Based Development*, 1(1/2): 6–24. doi: 10.1504/ IJKBD.2010.032583

Perry, B., Patel, Z., Norén Bretzer, Y. and Polk, M. (2018) 'Organising for coproduction: Local Interaction Platforms for urban sustainability', *Politics and Governance*, 6(1): 189–98. doi: 10.17645/pag.v6i1.1228

Pohl, C., Rist, S., Zimmermann, A., Fry, P., Gurung, G., Schneider, F., Speranza, C., Kiteme, B., Boillat, S., Serrano, E., Hirsch Hadorn, G. and Wiesmann, U. (2010) 'Researchers' roles in knowledge co-production: experience from sustainability research in Kenya, Switzerland, Bolivia and Nepal', *Science and Public Policy*, 37(4): 267–281.

Rittel, H.W.J. and Webber, M.M. (1973) 'Dilemmas in general theory of planning', *Policy Science*, 4: 155–69. doi: 10.1007/BF01405730

Robinson, J. (2011) 'Cities in a world of cities: the comparative gesture', *International Journal of Urban and Regional Research*, 35(1): 1–23. doi: 10.1111/j.1468-2427.2010.00982.x

Robinson, J. (2016) 'Comparative urbanism: new geographies and cultures of theorising the urban', *International Journal of Urban and Regional Research*, 40(1): 187–99. doi: 10.1016/ j.habitatint.2015.10.009

Roy, A. (2011) 'Urbanisms, worlding practices, and the theory of planning', *Planning Theory*, 10(1): 6–15. doi: 10.1177/ 1473095210386065

Roy, A. (2016) 'What is urban about critical urban theory?', *Urban Geography* 37(6): 810–23. doi: 10.1080/02723638.2015.1105485

Simon, D. (1984) 'Third world colonial cities in context: conceptual and theoretical approaches with particular reference to Africa', *Progress in Human Geography*, 8(4): 493–514. doi: 10.1177/030913258400800402

Simon, D. (1989) 'Colonial cities, postcolonial Africa and the world economy: a reinterpretation', *International Journal of Urban and Regional Research*, 13(1): 68–91. doi:10.1111/j.1468–2427.1989.tb00109.x

Simon, D. (1992) *Cities, Capital and Development: African Cities in the World Economy*, London: Belhaven Press.

Simon, D. (2015) 'Uncertain times, contested resources: discursive practices and lived realities in African urban environments', *City: Analysis Of Urban Trends, Culture, Theory, Policy, Action*, 19(2–3): 216–38, doi: 10.1080/13604813.2015.1018060

Simon, D., Palmer, H., Riise, J., Smit, W. and Valencia, S. (2018) 'The challenges of transdisciplinary knowledge production: from unilocal to comparative research', *Environment & Urbanization*, 30(2): 481–500. doi: 10.1177/0956247818787177

Walton, J. (1975) 'Introduction: problems of method and theory in comparative urban studies', *Urban Affairs Quarterly*, 11(1): 3–12. doi: 10.1177/107808747501100101

Voss, J. P. and Bornemann, P. (2011) 'The politics of reflexive governance: challenges for designing adaptive management and transition management', *Ecology and Society*, 16(2): 9–32.

THREE

Local projects retrofitted

Michael Oloko and Barry Ness

Introduction

This chapter presents and reflects on a process of international comparative and transdisciplinary co-production research referred to as 'local projects retrofitted', or, more precisely, retrofitting a comparative dimension on to an existing unilocal project. The intention is to demonstrate how the comparative process is understood and operationalised in one of the urban contexts to contribute towards sustainability and justice through joint research and problem solving for mutual benefit. We demonstrate how this may trigger surprising results and innovative solutions.

Such possibilities to relate and analyse situations from different cities, countries and regions make this process of retrofitting instructive for governments, private firms and donor agencies that are willing to facilitate access to and transfer good practice, knowledge and technologies between global South and North or South and South, to help meet international environmental obligations and commitments (UNCTAD, 2001; UN, 2004; UNEP, 2013). The focus on comparative dimensions helps to stimulate increased possibilities for sustainable urban change, enhance learning from both the positive and negative experiences in the cities being considered, and foster translocal links to promote sustainable urban change. This chapter draws on our experiences in developing and implementing the process of retrofitting a local project in Kenya with comparative dimensions drawn from ongoing developments in Sweden. In particular, we discuss the process of how a unilocal research project based in Kisumu (Kenya) was retrofitted, or adapted, to include comparative dimensions based on practices and experiences of a related project in Helsingborg (Sweden).

The sustainability challenge identified to illustrate this comparative process is solid waste management, which is one of the major global environmental problems and an important service all cities must provide. Indeed, the World Bank notes that a city that cannot effectively manage its waste is rarely able to manage other services such as health, education or transportation (Hoornweg and Bhada-Tata, 2012). The Solid Waste Management (SWM) comparative project, implemented by both the Kisumu Local Interaction Platform (KLIP) and Skåne Local Interaction Platform (SKLIP), respectively, is used to demonstrate how the process of retrofitting as a form of comparative transdisciplinary co-production takes place between the two regions. The project was prioritised by KLIP to identify and promote sustainable approaches to waste management in Kisumu city. The choice of the cities – Kisumu in Kenya and Helsingborg in Sweden – provides a global South–North perspective, making the process particularly relevant for development agencies that are keen on transferring good practices from one part of the world to another. Both cities have more or less similar goals: to achieve a more resource-efficient use, and ensure a clean and healthy environment as per the Kenya Constitution 2010 and the Swedish waste plan (Swedish Environmental Protection Agency, 2005; National Environmental Management Authority, 2014), but are at different levels of implementation within different socio-political and socio-technical contexts.

Solid waste management is a cross-cutting issue with impacts on 12 out of 17 Sustainable Development Goals (SDGs) of the 2030 Agenda for Sustainable Development, adopted by UN Member States in September 2015 (Wilson et al, 2015). This includes the three sustainability domains – ecology, economy and society – and in particular covers living conditions, sanitation, public health, marine and terrestrial ecosystems, access to decent jobs, and the sustainable use of natural resources (Rodic and Wilson, 2017). By comparing and contrasting different responses related to urban challenges in the two cities, we draw out experiences, lessons and knowledge of good practice that can influence future changes for the realisation of just cities. First, we present retrofitting, the different strategies *for* and experiences *of* building retrofitted comparative projects. Second, we discuss the comparative dimensions, and finally, we reflect on the main challenges and benefits of this process and comparative approach.

Retrofitting

Beyond the research methodological approach, introduced in the previous paragraphs, of retrofitting a comparative element on to an initially local project, the notion of 'retrofitting' existing urban environments has gained increased prominence within research and policy agendas in recent years (Sustainable Development Commission, 2010; Cole, 2012). As often understood at the level of buildings and neighbourhoods, the term 'urban retrofit' refers to reshaping the existing built environment, the networks and resources that flow through them and the physical fabric of the city (Bulkeley et al, 2011; Hodson and Marvin, 2016). As new sets of ecological, economic, social and political pressures are being exerted at the city level, the conceptual and empirical frame of urban retrofit extends from the domain of engineering and construction to encompass places, policy makers, finance, systems, natures, users and other interests and issues (Kelly, 2009). It is therefore not only about the technical fixes, add-ons or replacements, but also about a more fundamental retrofit of mindsets and behaviours – individually and organisationally – with new overarching socially and environmentally driven principles (Clarke et al, 2017). The approach of retrofitting therefore goes beyond the technical and economic feasibility issue to include global environmental governance as well as built environments and the role of cities within this (Hodson and Marvin, 2016). While cities are seen as being the source of many environmental and resource depletion problems, they are also recognised as major centres of population that offer huge potential opportunities in 'scaling up' responses to climate change and the need for energy efficiency, and are also seen as 'hubs' of innovative social practice and learning (Hodson and Marvin, 2010).

A critical challenge for contemporary urbanism is how cities develop the knowledge and capabilities to shape their built environment and urban infrastructure systematically in response to climate change and resource constraints (Hodson and Marvin, 2009; Hodson, 2014) across the entire ecological footprint of cities and the regions within which they are embedded (Hodson et al, 2012; May et al, 2013). There is hence a need to relate two strongly disconnected issues: 'what' is to be done to the city (for example, technical knowledge, targets, technological options), and 'how' measures will be implemented (for example, institutions, role of the citizens, governance) (Perry et al, 2013). The 'local projects retrofitted' typological category, in this case, compares two projects of the same theme but in different cities to identify what needs to be done and how, and builds on the positive experiences and lessons learnt during the comparative process. It is where existing research projects on a similar theme in different cities need retrofitting, or perhaps just a specific comparative add-on, to facilitate drawing conclusions about that particular theme from multiple contexts (Simon et al, 2018; see also Chapter Two of this volume).

Strategies for and experiences of building retrofitted comparative projects

This section is based on the understanding of the overall waste management system in general and the expectations at both local and global scales. It also explains how the two cities, Kisumu and Helsingborg, are brought together. Relevant aspects of the waste management situations in both cities are discussed to highlight the comparative dimensions. Waste governance, actors and institutions, waste management practices, facilities and technologies are some of the aspects of the urban waste management system considered, alongside climatic conditions potentially influencing actions towards sustainable waste management. Since they can influence actions towards waste management, the diverse climatic conditions are also considered.

The opportunities within the waste management value chain are primarily waste collection, transportation, material recovery and waste to energy systems, as described in the Kisumu County Integrated Development Plan 2018–22 (County Government of Kisumu, 2018). A principal focus was on the justification process for specific technological options, especially those at the end of the waste management chain, for instance, material recovery and waste-to-energy systems. These technological alternatives are not clearly understood in how they need to be implemented in the case of Kisumu, and replicating them (as will be described in Chapter Four) is not easily justifiable in relation to existing policies. There are fundamental questions to address: what are the feasible alternatives for Kisumu City other than the open dumping of solid waste? What solid waste handling alternatives exist that better incorporate principles of a circular economy? What collaborative approaches can best foster progress in these more sustainable directions?

Kisumu City generates approximately 400 tonnes of solid waste per day, only 20–25% of which was collected to the

Kachok open dump site until its recent closure by the county government. Of the total municipal solid waste collected, 65% is organic and another 27% is recyclable (County Government of Kisumu, 2015). Kisumu City authority collects waste directly from market areas and the central business district, while private waste actors collect waste from residential areas and business premises for a fee. Recycling centres in Kisumu are privately owned and are established to receive selected fractions of wastes. On the other hand, Helsingborg region (which includes six municipalities) generates 1,309 tonnes of waste per day, of which only 2% is landfilled, 59% is material recovered, 20% is treated biologically, and 18% is incinerated with energy recovery (Corvellec et al, 2011). In Helsingborg, however, contracted municipally owned companies (for example, NSR AB) collect waste within the city, but private companies can also be allowed, through competitive bidding, to collect waste from commercial or industrial establishments with extended producer responsibility. Solid waste is managed at well-established, municipality-owned recycling centres with necessary waste facilities. In addition, Verapark Circularity AB, a public–private partnership, has been established in Helsingborg, specialising in developing new or alternative products, such as furniture, from waste resources. In this comparative process a number of issues on waste management are worth noting. These include the level of waste recovery and land filling, the establishment and management of recycling centres, process of development of new products from waste resources, and the biological treatment of waste material as well as incineration with energy recovery.

To respond adequately and generate knowledge to address these critical aspects of waste management that every city must deal with, there was a need to find out how other cities were handling similar challenges, and to explore possibilities for cross-city learning. The first task was to determine which of the Mistra Urban Futures cities would be best placed to link up with Kisumu City in a way that will eventually add value to the project's activities. Helsingborg was deemed the most appropriate, with its advanced technology in waste management with both incineration and biological waste management processes, as well as its efforts to increase recycling and development of new products from waste resources. Relevant expertise from SKLIP was therefore sought to contribute to the comparative project and enable the local project to achieve its ultimate goal of contributing towards effective and sustainable environmental management for Kisumu. The objectives of the comparative project included mapping of waste management technological options and identifying the most appropriate options for solid waste management in Kisumu, testing the selected options for solid waste management in Kisumu and finally drawing up a roadmap for full implementation of the tested option.

The research process helped to foster a robust understanding of the waste management technologies and policies in both city contexts as a basis for the comparative dimensions. The research was undertaken by individual actors during the comparative project process from different societal realms familiar with their respective contexts and technologies. In the case of Kisumu, it involved researchers and actors who participated in an earlier KLIP project under the theme of marketplaces, that identified waste management as an area of interest (Ngusale et al, 2017), which eventually formed the basis of this comparative project implemented by both KLIP and SKLIP. From SKLIP, a practitioner based at Verapark, in conjunction with researchers from Lund University, made up the team in the new comparative approach. The proposed waste management solutions that were considered relevant during the project, for instance, management of organic waste through biogas technology, included broader institutional arrangements, individual socio-political situations and viable technologies for Kisumu. Regular communication between the teams involved consultations through Skype meetings, joint workshops in both Kisumu and Helsingborg, presentations and meetings at international conferences in Kisumu and Cape Town, study visits to waste management facilities (including the Kachok open dump in Kisumu, residential areas in both cities, bio-reactor landfills in Helsingborg, and waste recycling centres and incineration plants in Helsingborg), and presentations of plausible waste management options for Kisumu in two stake-holder workshops. The comparative project team was therefore constituted to draw on experiences and practices for mutual learning about what lessons from Helsingborg might be rele-vant for Kisumu but also how Kisumu's situation and approach might prove instructive for Helsingborg, which has been locked into its capital-intensive, hi-tech approach for over 20 years.

Waste management policies in Kenya aim to increase the value of waste through industrial processing activities to produce useful products or to derive energy from waste resources through reusing, recycling or composting (National Environmental Management Authority, 2014; Ministry of Environment and Forestry, 2018). Therefore, policies are con-sistent with the solid waste management hierarchy: prevent, reduce, recycle, recover, treat and dispose. In Helsingborg, waste management activities are dictated by European Union (EU) and more targeted Swedish legislation, also guided by the waste hierarchy – promoting waste management efforts upwards towards prevention, reuse and recycling. Anaerobic digestion of organic wastes, resulting in biogas production and digestate as recycling operations, has been prioritised above waste incineration and co-generation, with high level energy recovery (Article 2 [6] of Commission Decision 2011). Incineration with limited energy recovery and landfilling rank lowest (UNEP, 2013). This is not consistent with some trends in other European cities, nor with other Swedish cities.

Within the comparative research team and the collaborative processes, various deliberate actions and strategies were taken to facilitate learning and knowledge generation. For example, the Verapark representative was included as a part of the team to augment learning about new/alternative products from waste resources that could be pursued in Kisumu, including compost manure, biogas and briquettes. This also helped to promote the creation of spaces to develop and test innovative ideas. In particular, the city of Kisumu has allocated a piece of land through a temporary occupation licence to a private waste actor to support research and demonstration activities on different waste management technologies. The activities at the site include briquetting technology testing, composting and anaerobic biodigestion of organic waste resources to produce biogas and biofertiliser. In addition, there is the direct link with another actor, Zingira, a community-based organisation, for the development and improvement of locally produced sanitary pads from water hyacinth. The demonstration site, therefore, has become part and parcel of the waste management research project in Kisumu. The appropriate waste-to-energy system for Kisumu has also been considered with reference to the diverse experiences and somehow the focus is strongly on management of organic waste, through anaerobic processes to produce biogas and biofertiliser. Pilot demonstrations at both the Kibuye Market and Nyamasaria area in Kisumu City are focused on promoting this technology of waste management.

In one of the stakeholder workshops held in Kisumu in 2018 and attended by officials from both the city and the county, a waste governance management model based on the configuration of NSR in Sweden was proposed. It would involve the city authority contracting a private company to manage and maintain the city's waste facilities. The multi-stakeholder Kisumu Waste Actors' Network, which is a creation of earlier research projects on waste management, has positioned itself to manage at least one of the waste recycling/transfer/recovery stations to be created in the wards within the city. As a result of international policies to increase environmental sustainability, more consideration is being given to waste recycling and biodigestion as opposed to incineration, which is popular in the global North. This presents divergent priorities between the two regions, which may be worth considering later.

Comparative dimensions during the process

Choice of city for comparison

Finding relevant participants elsewhere is necessary for any comparative transdisciplinary co-production project. The project considered Helsingborg as a relevant city for comparison based on the existing Mistra Urban Futures LIP network, the waste management situation in Kisumu and the possible areas for improvement. Its advanced technical waste management infrastructure of diverse waste management options of both high-tech incineration plants operating alongside modern biogas systems (in form of both bio-cell units and bioreactors in the landfills) provides an opportunity to study and understand the operations of individual waste management technologies, and the hybrid system, as guidance towards future sustainable solutions in waste management in Kisumu.

Targeted expertise of the research team

Another vital component of the process was to include individuals with specialised knowledge. In considering the project's need for expertise and experience based on geographical locations and practices, the research team was strengthened by bringing in a highly knowledgeable and experienced researcher on the use of biological processes for waste management and, as mentioned, a practitioner from Verapark to reinforce the component of developing new/alternative products from waste resources.

Setting up a research demonstration site

The establishment of a designated facility to test various waste management technologies was key to this research process. The expertise from SKLIP and experience from Verapark demonstrated the possibilities of developing alternative products from waste resources. Learning from Verapark informed the experiments in Kibuye in Kisumu with the help of one of the waste actor organisations – the community-based organisation (CBO) Kibuye Waste Management – which was represented in the research team. The temporary occupation licence that has since been provided by the city of Kisumu shows formal commitment of the local government to support this process. This project therefore has played the role of reframing waste as an economic resource through the development and testing of products from waste resources, that is co-development of prototypes.

Real scientific evidence

Developing an appropriate waste management strategy requires evidence to support proposed technologies or management options. This responsibility lies with the research team to furnish the policy makers with such information. Preliminary findings of the research were consolidated and presented in a stakeholder workshop in Kisumu, attended by practitioners as well as local government officials. It showed that the benefits of biological processes for solid waste management outweigh those for incineration. This was based on the opportunities for promoting a circular economy, support to livelihoods and environment sustainability concerns. More evidence regarding these possibilities is to be gathered in the ongoing experiments from the research demonstration site at Kibuye Market.

Analysis of waste management technologies

Despite the inclusion of experts and demonstration facilities into the collaborative process, additional research participants were necessary. To provide more concrete scientific evidence regarding the viability of the different technologies, additional researchers from Sweden were invited into the group to perform a joint multi-criteria analysis. This provided more targeted knowledge on the different waste management options to aid decision-making processes at city level.

Waste governance and networks

Building formal working relationships throughout the process with the local authorities and networks among the waste actors is important for effective waste governance. This has been carried out with the support of research activities of the comparative project. Kisumu City authority has issued a temporary occupation licence to Kibuye Waste Management CBO for demonstration of waste management practices at Kibuye Market, showing a working relationship with the waste actor. A relationship between Verapark and Zingira CBO in Kisumu has also been established and it is based on development and production of sanitary pads from water hyacinth for both local and export markets, including Sweden. The CBO representative visited Sweden twice in 2018 to explore this further.

Privatisation of waste management services in the city

In many cities, the waste management facilities are owned by the local authorities but leased out to private companies through contracts. The local authorities therefore carry out the supervisory roles, as noted in the case of the NSR company in Sweden. This research project has also considered possibilities of such a governance system for Kisumu. It proposes the establishment of waste management facilities by the city and the need to assess the benefits versus costs of privatising the management of these facilities through lease agreements with the private companies (see, for example, the various perspectives in Zapata Campos and Hall, 2013). To create incentives for various waste actors, including community groups and networks, the research team also presented a business model with business opportunities based on provision of waste management services and products from waste resources for sustainability at the local scale.

Benefits

The comparative project has brought together groups of researchers from Kenyan and Swedish universities with diverse backgrounds and relevant expertise. Practitioners and community members participated in the research activities, giving their views. Other organisations, for example, the international non-governmental organisation (NGO) Practical Action, also contributed through related projects with waste pickers on the Kachok dump site in Kisumu before its closure. The process therefore allowed for the integration of various similar projects, experts, organisations, practitioners and other stakeholders, resulting in the consolidation of resources, efforts and sustained engagement. Although it took time to constitute such a research team, the discussion became rich and generated a sense of shared ownership of the project, with trials taking place at the same time, for example, at Kibuye demonstration site with biodigesters for management of organic waste.

The approach in this comparative project has allowed for transdisciplinary co-production of knowledge in Kisumu and led to discussion of various solid waste management technologies, both simple and sophisticated. This, in turn, led to the formulation of proposals for managing organic waste through biodigestion and production of both biogas and biofertiliser as the locally most appropriate solution. This, therefore, challenged the modernist notion that the way forward should simply be to adopt advanced technology from the global North. Increased environmental sustainability does not necessarily coincide with the level of investment or the level of sophistication of any given technology. The European

Commission favours waste prevention and recycling of waste that also includes anaerobic digestion with biogas production and a digestate as biofertiliser (European Commission, 2017). For increased environmental sustainability, incineration may not be the best option, even in Europe, despite its potential for district heating as a co-benefit. However, it provides a quick-fix solution, and most African cities including Kisumu think of it positively (Oteng-Ababio et al, 2013). Accordingly, this project has demonstrated how bringing all the stakeholders together in a co-productive relationship can arrive at locally appropriate and sustainable outcomes.

Learning through participation, demonstrations and experimentations is important for testing different strategies, technologies and products, and enabling their benefits to be more widely understood. Issuing a temporary occupation licence to the demonstration site shows the interest/desire of the local authority to achieve effective and sustainable solid waste management in the city. Methodologically, the approach adds to the establishment of urban development processes that are more inclusive where a variety of voices are heard, therefore contributing to the realisation of just cities.

Like many other African cities, Kisumu still has greater opportunities to test different technologies of waste management, which can later be beneficial to the global North. What can the global South contribute to the world in this context? One answer is a simple waste management technology, fully tested and functional in urban areas like Kisumu City. Policies in the North do not allow experimentation and testing of some products from waste resources, while long-term technological lock-in from past decisions, such as investments in capital-intensive incinerators or other equipment, limits the ability to respond to new technologies, understandings or opportunities (Unruh and Carrillo-Hermosilla, 2006; Corvellec and Hultman 2012; Corvellec et al, 2012). This may prompt a review of past decisions, and hence a change in policies, to allow for more opportunities of interventions.

Limitations encountered during the project

While the process of comparative research is beneficial in many respects, building an international team is time-consuming. This involves identifying the collaborating city as well as the expertise and the relevant organisations with which to partner. To some extent, it also requires prior understanding of the prevailing situations in other cities, in order to establish the relevance and possible comparative dimensions based on previously identified gaps. Even though information and communications technology has made it easy to discuss issues between distant places, it is still necessary to meet and undertake joint collaborative research activities, which may be expensive, hence compromising the effectiveness of implementation of the research activities throughout the process and therefore quality of the findings.

The research team comprised individuals from different institutions with different mandates. By participating in the research activities, the expectation to fulfill these mandates, some of which are not research-oriented (for example, development or marketing in nature), is difficult to achieve. This resulted in discouragement and withdrawal of some members.

The unexpected actions of the county/city government to evacuate waste materials from Kachok dump site and later close it in August 2019, before any comprehensive solid waste management strategy of the kind being explored in this project could be implemented, and to explain the implications, has created new challenges of what will happen to the waste in the short term. The Kachok dump site had been earmarked for demonstration of gas collection and composting, but this did not take place.

This category in the typology of comparative research – retrofitting of local projects as a comparative strategy – involves cities with different socio-technical operating systems, such as Helsingborg with technologically advanced waste management technologies, and Kisumu with non-existent or rudimentary technologies. The collaborative process can create the impression that one city cannot learn or benefit from the practices of the other, creating lack of motivation and interest for one city team, but the experience reported here has demonstrated otherwise.

Conclusion

Our conclusions relate both to the substantive research topic of SWM and to the research experience of undertaking an innovative comparative project on local projects retrofitted.

Regarding SWM, Kenya represents an emblematic global South perspective of being at the lowest technological levels of implementation of the SWM hierarchy (UNEP, 2013), with open dumping sites and low levels of separation and recycling at source. Conversely, Helsingborg has pursued an approach comprising recycling, anaerobic digestion for organic fractions and incineration with energy recovery for solid waste streams. The approach helps to narrow the gap between policy expectations and practice, even though the trend does not seem to be consistent with EU policies. The research outcomes from the transdisciplinary co-production research process, therefore, favours recycling alongside biological treatment, with incineration last. Provision of basic services, like waste management services, needs to respond to the emerging complex environmental challenges resulting from the existing methodologies, approaches and technologies in various regions of the world. Retrofitting our way towards a sustainable future, both in terms of the mindsets of decision makers and individual behavioural change, should therefore be guided by a universal agenda. This, therefore, interrogates divergent local as well as regional policies and practices, and how they respond to the global agendas such as the SDGs.

Different countries adopt diverse approaches to SWM, and are at different technological levels of implementation, ranging from traditional and/or informal means and methods to advanced sophisticated technologies, but everywhere now favours an emerging resource recovery waste regime as well as policies that promote resource recovery and recycling over disposal through landfills (Gille, 2013). Waste management is part of the critical infrastructure that greatly improves living conditions in cities. However, when such infrastructure performs well, it tends to be taken for granted and therefore becomes invisible until it loses relevance or becomes obsolete (Graham and Thrift, 2007). To understand how to overcome 'lock-in' situations and facilitate systems change will be critical to achieving sustainability (Lomas, 2009; Lowe, 2009). Lessons drawn from such collaborative work can contribute to diminishing this knowledge gap.

This chapter has explored retrofitting as one transdisciplinary co-production process to foster sustainable urban change on complex challenges. Experiences have shown that careful planning must be done to ensure the right project partners participate in the collaborative work. It is also important that individual participants with the right technical and socio-political knowledge participate to help guide the knowledge co-production processes in plausible directions. Establishing demonstration and pilot projects was also an important part of the process, as they were avenues to test the feasibility of specific waste treatment technologies and were an effective way to build supportive evidence for decision makers and the general public. Finally, inclusion of other key actors such as government decision makers and the private sector early on in the transdisciplinary co-production process were also key in creating buy-in and fostering mutual trust among the different partners.

Acknowledgements

The authors would like to acknowledge and thank Dusan Raicevic and Torleif Bramryd for their contributions to the Mistra Urban Futures solid waste management comparative project.

References

Bulkeley, H., Castán-Broto, V., Hodson, M. and Marvin, S. (eds) (2011) *Cities and Low Carbon Transitions*, Routledge: London.

Clarke, S.F., Nawaz, W., Skelhorn, C, and Amato, A. (2017) 'Towards a more sustainable waste management in Qatar: retrofitting mindsets and changing behaviours', *QScience Connect, Shaping Qatar's Sustainable Built Environment* 2017:qgbc.4. doi: http://dx.doi.org/10.5339/ connect.2017.qgbc.4

Cole, R. (2012) 'Regenerative design and development: current theory and practice', *Building Research and Information*, 40(1): 1–6. doi: 10.1080/09613218.2012

Corvellec, H. and Hultman, J. (2012) 'From "less landfilling" to "wasting less": societal narratives, socio-materiality, and organizations', *Journal of Organizational Change Management*, 25(2): 297–314.

Corvellec, H., Bramryd, T. and Hultman, J. (2011) 'The business model of solid waste management in Sweden – a case study of two municipally-owned companies', *Waste Management & Research*, 30(5): 512–18. doi:10.1177/0734242X11427944

Corvellec, H., Zapata Campos, M.J. and Zapata, P. (2012) 'Infrastructures, lock-in, and sustainable urban development: the case of waste incineration in the Göteborg Metropolitan Area', *Journal of Cleaner Production*, 50(1): 32–9. Available from: http://dx.doi.org/10.1016/j.jclepro.2012.12.009

County Government of Kisumu (2015) *Kisumu Integrated Solid Waste Management Strategy 2015–2025*, Kisumu: County Government of Kisumu.

County Government of Kisumu (2018) *Kisumu County Integrated Development Plan II (CIDP 2018–2022)*, Kisumu: County Government of Kisumu.

European Commission (2017) *Communication from the Commission to the European Parliament, the Council, the European Economic and Social Committee and the Committee of the Regions, 26.1.2017 COM (2017) 34 final*, Brussels: European Commission.

European Union (2011) Article 2 (6) of Commission Decision 2011/753/EU establishing rules and calculation methods for verifying compliance with the targets set in Article 11(2) of Directive 2008/98/EC of the European Parliament and of the Council. OJ L 310 of 25.11.2011.

Gille, Z. (2013) 'From risk to waste: global food waste regimes', *The Sociological Review*, 60, S2: 27–46. doi: 10.1111/1467-954X.12036

Graham, S. and Thrift, N. (2007) 'Out of order: understanding repair and maintenance', *Theory, Culture & Society*, 24(3): 1–25.

Hodson, M. (2014) *Remaking the Material Fabric of the City? Why it Matters, How it is Being Done, and What this Tells us*, Report for the Greater Manchester Local Interaction Platform of Mistra Urban Futures, Manchester: Mistra Urban Futures.

Hodson, M. and Marvin, S. (2009) 'Urban ecological security: a new urban paradigm?', *International Journal of Urban and Regional Research*, 33(1): 193–215.

Hodson, M. and Marvin, S. (2010) 'Can cities shape sociotechnical transitions and how would we know if they were?', *Research Policy*, 39: 477–85.

Hodson, M. and Marvin, S. (2016) *Retrofitting Cities: Priorities, Governance and Experimentation*, London: Routledge.

Hodson, M., Marvin, S., Robinson, B. and Swilling, M. (2012) 'Reshaping urban infrastructure: material flow analysis and transitions analysis in an urban context', *Journal of Industrial Ecology*, 16(6): 789–800.

Hoornweg, D. and Bhada-Tata, P. (2012) *What a Waste: A Global Review of Solid Waste Management*, Urban Development Series Knowledge Papers No. 15, Washington, DC: World Bank. Available from: https://openknowledge.worldbank.org/handle/10986/17388 (License: CC BY 3.0 IGO).

Kelly, M. (2009) 'Retrofitting the existing UK building stock', *Building Research and Information*, 37(2): 196–200.

Lomas, K. (2009) 'Decarbonising national housing stocks: barriers and measurement', *Building Research and Information*, 37(2): 187–91.

Lowe, R. (2009) 'Policy and strategy challenges for climate change and building stocks', *Building Research and Information*, 37(2): 206–12.

May, T., Hodson, M., Marvin, S. and Perry, B., (2013) 'Achieving "Systemic" Urban Retrofit: A Framework for Action'. In W. Swan and P. Brown, (eds) *Retrofitting the Built Environment*. Chichester: John Wiley and Sons, pp 7–19.

Ministry of Environment and Forestry (2018) *National Sustainable Waste Management Policy*, Sessional Paper No. X, September, Nairobi: Ministry of Environment and Forestry.

National Environmental Management Authority (2014) *The National Solid Waste Management Strategy* Nairobi: National Environmental Management Authority.

Ngusale, G., Oloko, M., Agong, S. and Nyakinya, B. (2017) 'Energy recovery from municipal solid waste', *Energy Sources Part A: Recovery, Utilization and Environmental Effects*, 39(16): 1807–14. doi: 10.1080/15567036.2017.1376007

Oteng-Ababio, M., Melara E.J. and Gabbay, O. (2013) 'Solid waste management in African cities: sorting the facts from fads in Accra, Ghana', *Habitat International*, 39: 96–104. doi: 10.1016/j.habitatint.2012.10.010

Perry, B., May, T., Marvin, S. and Hodson, M. (2013) Re-thinking sustainable knowledge-based urbanism through active intermediation. In Anderson, H.T. and Atkinson, R. (eds) *The Production and Use of Urban Knowledge: European Experiences*. Dordrecht: Springer, pp 157–167.

Rodic, L. and Wilson, D. (2017) 'Resolving governance issues to achieve priority Sustainable Development Goals related to solid waste management in developing countries', *Sustainability*, 9: 404. doi:10.3390/su9030404

Simon, D., Palmer, H., Riise, J., Smit, W. and Valencia, S. (2018) 'The challenges of transdisciplinary knowledge production: from unilocal to comparative research', *Environment & Urbanization*, 30(2): 481–500. doi: 10.1177/0956247818787177

Sustainable Development Commission (2010) *The Future is Local: Empowering Communities to Improve their Neighbourhoods*, London: Sustainable Development Commission.

Swedish Environmental Protection Agency (2005) *A Strategy for Sustainable Waste Management: Sweden's Waste Plan*, Stockholm: Swedish Environmental Protection Agency.

UN (United Nations) (2004) *Facilitating Transfer of Technology to Developing Countries: A Survey of Home-Country Measures*, UNCTAD Series on Technology Transfer and Development, New York, NY and Geneva: UN.

UNCTAD (United Nations Conference on Trade and Development) (2001) *Compendium of International Arrangements on Technology Transfer: Selected Instruments*, UNCTAD/ITE/IPC/Misc.5, Geneva: UN.

UNEP (United Nations Environment Programme) (2013) *Guidelines for National Waste Management Strategies: Moving from Challenges to Opportunities*, Nairobi: UNEP.

Unruh, G.C. and Carrillo-Hermosilla, J. (2006) 'Globalizing carbon lock-in', *Energy Policy*, 34 (10): 1185–97.

Wilson, D.C., Rodic, L., Modak, P., Soos, R., Carpintero Rogero, A., Velis, C., Iyer, M. and Simonett, O. (2015) *Global Waste Management Outlook*, Osaka: UNEP International Environment Technology Centre.

Zapata Campos, M.J. and Hall, C.M. (eds) (2013) *Organising Waste in the City: International Perspectives on Narratives and Practice*, Bristol: Policy Press.

FOUR

Replicating projects for comparative research: Mistra Urban Futures' experiences with comparative work on knowledge exchange, food and transport

Warren Smit, Elma Durakovic, Rike Sitas, Magnus Johansson, Gareth Haysom,

Mirek Dymitrow, Karin Ingelhag and Shelley Kotze

Introduction

This chapter discusses three comparative projects that were all, at least partially, created through the replication of research across the Mistra Urban Futures cities. At the start of Phase Two of Mistra Urban Futures, we developed a typology of six possible models of how comparative transdisciplinary knowledge co-production could take place across multiple cities (see Chapter Two), and the second of these approaches was identified as 'local projects replicated'. This is where particular successful projects initiated in individual cities had been, or were intended to be, replicated in other cities, thus opening up possibilities for cross-city comparison.

As it turned out, three Mistra Urban Futures comparative projects were partially or entirely based on projects that had been replicated in other cities: the knowledge exchange project, the suite of linked food comparative projects, and Transport and Sustainable Urban Development comparative project. This chapter draws on our practical experience in developing and implementing these comparative projects. First, we discuss the issue of 'replication' and the different ways that this can occur. Second, we discuss the initial work on these themes (knowledge exchange, food, transport) that formed the basis for the development of these particular comparative projects. Third, we discuss the complex processes through which this work assembled into comparative projects. Finally, we reflect on the challenges and benefits of 'replicating' projects for comparative research.

Replication

Traditionally, the replication of research has been key in ensuring that empirical results are robust enough to serve as a basis for theorisation (Amir and Sharon, 1990). Replication has thus long been considered 'the cornerstone of science', with reproducibility of research often being synonymous with scientific integrity (Moonesinghe et al, 2007; Simons, 2014). Approaches to the replication of research vary considerably across research disciplines and fields of study (Repko and Szostak, 2016). Broadly, however, the replication of research has two main objectives: reproducibility, that is the replication of the same method to obtain the same results; and generalisability, that is showing that the method works in different contexts (Amir and Sharon, 1990).

Some scholars are of the view that social and life sciences are currently facing a 'replication crisis', with the results of many quantitative scientific studies being difficult or impossible to replicate or reproduce on subsequent investigation, either by independent researchers or by the original researchers themselves (Pashler and Wagenmakers, 2012; Schooler, 2014; Smith, 2017). This replication crisis is seen as largely driven by a failure to adhere to good scientific practice and the desperation to 'publish or perish' (Begley and Ioannidis, 2015). Whereas the replication of quantitative research and many technological development interventions are of necessity fairly rigid, without much scope for local adaptation, qualitative research and social development interventions are usually generally more open-ended, and can be more easily adapted to different contexts.

In this chapter, we discuss how different projects were 'replicated' across the different Mistra Urban Futures cities and were then used as a basis for comparative research. It is important to note that this replication occurred in many different ways:

- Replication of quantitative research, such as the food security household surveys in the Consuming Urban Poverty project. This type of replication had the least amount of adaptation to local context (but even this usually involved some changes in terminology, translation to other languages, and so on).
- Replication of qualitative research, using the same questions and methods as in the Transport and Sustainable Urban Development project. This type of replication usually had much more adaptation to the local context.
- Replication of broad objectives through context-specific social development interventions, such as the local government–university knowledge exchange programmes implemented in Cape Town and Skåne, and the food security strategy work undertaken in a number of different cities. Although the overall objectives were replicated, the methods and substance of the work were usually extensively adapted to suit the local context.

It is therefore important to note that, as explained in Chapter Two, when we talk about replication in the context of the

Mistra Urban Futures comparative projects, it was usually the replication of broad objectives rather than the exact replication of detailed methodologies and identical empirical matter. This was suited to comparative case research, which is essentially about inductive enquiry into agreements and differences between different cases, and the reasons/causes for these (Abu-Lughod, 2007). In some of the Mistra Urban Futures comparative projects, as discussed in the following sections, the comparative research projects were focused on analysing and understanding the different methods used in different places rather than comparing similarities and differences in research findings. This is therefore very different from replication in positivist science.

Mistra Urban Futures' initial work on knowledge exchange, food and transport

Mistra Urban Futures' research work focused on the co-production of knowledge for urban justice and urban sustainability, and on how best to bridge divides between academic research and policy/practice to co-produce relevant knowledge. One key area of work was knowledge exchange between academia and local government, and the creation of a cohort of people who could work across this divide. Other key areas of work related to different aspects of urban justice, such as urban food security and urban transport. Both of these issues are key dimensions of urban inequality and also have strong links to the urban sustainability agenda.

Knowledge exchange

Since its establishment in 2007, the African Centre for Cities at the University of Cape Town had partnered closely with the City of Cape Town, and had identified a number of key topics for collaboration between City officials, university researchers and other stakeholders. This resulted in the establishment of the CityLab programme (Anderson et al, 2013; Smit et al, 2015; Culwick et al, 2019). Although very successful in producing new research and developing new policies, obtaining the long-term commitment of city officials was a continual challenge, due to understaffing and constant internal institutional and urban crises with which officials needed to deal. After the African Centre for Cities joined Mistra Urban Futures in 2010, as the anchor for the Cape Town Local Interaction Platform (CTLIP), it was decided to develop a more structured programme to create a cohort of researchers that could straddle the worlds of academic research and local government policy/practice and thus help contribute to both the development of policy-relevant research and research-informed policies. The CTLIP Knowledge Transfer Programme was therefore launched in 2012 (Miszczak and Patel, 2018).

The first component of the Knowledge Transfer Programme was the embedding of PhD researchers within the City of Cape Town for three years at a time, to work for the City (typically for 50–60% of their time) on policy/research on a particular theme while simultaneously doing academic research on the same theme, in this way helping both to inject cutting-edge research into local government policy processes (and significantly adding to local government capacity), while also helping ensure that research on local government is based on the realities that officials face. In all, seven PhD researchers were embedded in the City of Cape Town, five of them for three years each and two of them for two years each. The topics they have worked on are: climate change adaptation and mitigation; the green economy; energy governance; understanding the urban economy spatially; transport justice; inclusionary housing; and cultural planning.

The second component of the Knowledge Transfer Programme was an official exchange programme for City of Cape Town officials to get up to two months of 'academic leave' each to spend at the University of Cape Town writing up and reflecting on their practical experiences of the City, and undertaking reviews of relevant literature so they could relate their work to theory and the existing body of knowledge. Practitioners were paired with relevant academic writing partners to write journal articles and book chapters on their work. The officials' exchange programme enabled officials to document and reflect on their work (which was something that had previously seldom happened), and also enabled them to engage with the academic literature and think about the implications for their daily practice (for example, see Scott et al, 2019).

In 2016, the Skåne Local Interaction Platform (SKLIP), centred in Malmö and Lund, joined Mistra Urban Futures and also initiated a knowledge exchange programme. The three universities in the region – Lund, Malmö and the Alnarp campus of the Swedish University of Agricultural Sciences – joined forces to find new ways to support municipal strategic challenges connected to sustainable development, primarily with regard to planning and building activities. The title of the programme, When Municipalities set the Research Agenda, indicates that the ambition in the long run is to question the power dynamic between academia and municipalities when it comes to setting the research agendas. The overall purpose of this project is to explore if and how a particular form of promoting organisational learning, which we term public sector-led research, can contribute to cross-departmental learning in the municipalities and, in turn, enable sustainable urban development and innovation.

As part of this programme, officials from various municipalities have had time freed up to undertake part-time PhDs on the themes they work on. Although broadly the same as the Knowledge Transfer Programme in that it has created a cohort of researchers who straddle local government and academia, the different context has resulted in the details of the programme being quite different. The project has four 'municipal PhDs'. The PhD students are supported by main supervisors from the universities and co-supervisors from the municipality. Two of the PhD students are placed in the City of Malmö (one of them is doing a PhD through the University of Malmö and one through the University of Lund), and the other two are based in small municipalities elsewhere in Skåne County: one is in Staffanstorp (undertaking a PhD through the Swedish Agricultural University) and one is in Östra Göinge municipality.

Food

The Kisumu Local Interaction Platform (KLIP) had a focus on food since its inception, as marketplaces (which play a central role in the food systems of African cities) was one of its two main priorities during Phase One of Mistra Urban Futures. In 2014, KLIP began collaborating with CTLIP on research on urban food security and in 2016 it began collaborating with the Gothenburg Local Interaction Platform (GOLIP) on the *Stadslandet* project (discussed later in this section).

The African Centre for Cities has undertaken research on urban food security since 2011, in recognition of the fact that urban food insecurity levels remain stubbornly high, particularly in Africa, and because urban food systems are a useful lens for understanding and addressing issues of urban poverty and inequality. This food work initially focused on Cape Town (for example, collaboration with the City of Cape Town on a citywide food strategy) and in other cities in Africa as part of the African Food Security Urban Network. In 2014, a portion of this urban food security research became part of the Mistra Urban Futures research agenda when the Consuming Urban Poverty project was initiated. This project, which involved collaboration between CTLIP and KLIP, focused on understanding urban food systems and urban food insecurity in secondary cities in Africa, through undertaking household food security surveys and mapping and analysing urban food retail systems (Battersby and Watson, 2018; Opiyo and Agong, 2018; Opiyo et al, 2018a, 2018b).

GOLIP's involvement in food-related work was mainly through the Urban Rural Gothenburg project (*Stadslandet* in Swedish), a three-year (2017–19) European Union-funded project for sustainable development based within Business Region Gothenburg – the city's wholly owned company for business development – rather than at one of the city's universities. The project's overarching aim was to create improved conditions for green innovation and green business development between the city and the countryside. Three of the sub-projects relate closely to food. First, Angered Farmstead is a new development and knowledge centre for urban farming in northern Gothenburg. The centre offers both theoretical and practical training, focusing on efficient, intensive, small-scale and economically sustainable vegetable cultivation for the urban market.

Second, Locally Produced Food for Public Kitchens is a sub-project aiming to supply the public kitchens of the City of Gothenburg (mostly schools) with locally produced lamb meat. A farm has been contracted to produce lamb meat for Gothenburg's preschools. Third, the Applied Food Strategy for Gothenburg is an ongoing investigation on behalf of the City of Gothenburg to provide suggestions as to how Gothenburg's local food system can contribute to a sustainable and healthy food supply for the entire Gothenburg metropolitan area, while at the same time reducing the city's environmental impact beyond the national borders.

During Phase Two of Mistra Urban Futures, the Sheffield–Manchester Local Interaction Platform (SMLIP) also worked on food, creating a communications hub to assist, develop and support local initiatives that self-organise to share learning and skills and resources. SMLIP then began collaborating with the Gothenburg LIP (GOLIP) on the Self-organising Action for Food Equity (SAFE) project. The project's aim was to assist in the development of local food strategies in Sheffield, Greater

Manchester and Gothenburg. The key problem statement was that in such a process there was generally a lack of understanding on how best to organise, harmonise and capitalise on the energy of separate projects. This was in part informed by the fact that the food system spans social, ecological, economic, political, cultural, technical and climatic arenas. One strand of the project was to evaluate and share insights on how expertise and information in urban food systems is collected, presented and shared using 'digital infrastructure'.

As can be seen, the Mistra Urban Futures food work expanded through a series of processes: the replication of a food security survey methodology from Cape Town to Kisumu; the expansion of the *Stadslandet* project to include involvement in Kisumu; and the expansion of food strategy work to include three locations in the UK and Sweden as part of the SAFE project. Although these projects broadly shared the same objectives, they went about achieving these in very different ways in different contexts, with a range of different perspectives and approaches. Broadly, in the global North cities there was a focus on the localisation of food systems, whereas in the two global South cities there was a focus on improving urban food security.

In the *Stadslandet* project, which involved a range of sub-projects, it was found that the quality of social relationships between all stakeholders and actors involved can have a big impact on the success of projects, and these factors can also affect the replication of projects. The *Stadslandet* team identified six criteria according to which the sub-projects' success or failure was evaluated, grouped into structural and psychological factors (Dymitrow and Brauer, 2018). Structural factors are those shaping the design of the project: explicit formal assignment of duties/responsibilities to actors in the project; allocation of resources, for example in terms of staffing and funds, to a project; and leadership of the project. As these factors consolidate in structured relations between professionals, they are predominantly collective. Psychological factors relate to the cognitive processes of the human mind, which are ever-present in all our everyday activities, including the running of projects. Psychological factors were identified as incentive, ability and will. These vary from person to person and are therefore largely individual, although they, of course, intersect with structural factors. In the *Stadslandet* project, it was found that successful projects scored highly for all (or most) dimensions. Projects that that generally rated poorly in terms of structural factors and/or psychological factors performed poorly.

Transport

There were various transport-related projects undertaken during Phase One and the early stages of Phase Two of Mistra Urban Futures: the Urban Stations Communities project in the Gothenburg region; Urban Stations Communities work in Kisumu; and work on transit-oriented development undertaken in Cape Town as part of the Knowledge Transfer Programme.

The Urban Station Communities project is a long-term project within GOLIP focused on knowledge about the complexities in planning for the development of communities around railway stations (Ranhagen et al, 2017). The objective is to revitalise and support municipalities' regular planning processes to stimulate the building of an efficient transport system in the Gothenburg region, with dense station communities that have a good quality-of-living environment. A wide range of municipalities and other partners work in several sub-projects. Kimusu LIP (KLIP) is engaging with the Urban Station Communities as an approach to the location and construction of a new railway station in Kisumu as a result of the extension of a Chinese-built Standard Gauge Railway to Kisumu. This will result in the creation of a new station with direct impact on the community in the new location. The site of the former railway station (the old railway has closed down) on the shore of Lake Victoria, close to the city centre, also needs to be redeveloped.

As part of the second phase of CTLIP's Knowledge Transfer Programme, from 2015 onwards, there was a focus on transit-oriented development (TOD), which had become the priority of the City of Cape Town in its efforts to spatially transform the sprawling and segregated urban pattern of the city. The strategy is essentially about creating dense, mixed-use corridors along the main public transport corridors in Cape Town. Two embedded researchers were appointed to work on various aspects of the City's TOD strategy. CTLIP thus also became involved in research on transport. Although broadly similar to the Urban Station Communities project in that it focused on spatial transformation around public transport, in practice it was a bit different in that bus-rapid transit, rather than rail, has increasingly been seen as the key form of public transport in Cape Town, so the main focus was on bus corridors.

The comparative projects

Knowledge exchange

The purpose of the Knowledge Transfer comparative project is to learn from experiences of the knowledge transfer programmes in Cape Town (Knowledge Transfer Programme) and Skåne (When Municipalities set the Research Agenda) in order to implement innovative ways of working in our respective countries. The focus is on comparing different kinds of partnerships in order to strengthen collaborative work between the state, universities and society, and try those methods in practice in Sweden and South Africa. The research has three priorities:

- exploring different state–university–society partnerships and collaborations, with a certain focus on how they function as brokering communities;

- deepening theoretical understanding of conditions for co-production and collaborative and comparative research in different national and institutional contexts;
- developing methods for successful transfer and implementation of good practice in university–society collaboration between two different national contexts, in this case Sweden and South Africa.

The two teams, from Cape Town and Skåne, undertook a process of exchange and collaborative research and reflection, including a series of workshops and interviews with municipal officials undertaken by the visiting teams. A team from Sweden visited Cape Town in June 2018, and then a team from Cape Town visited Malmö in September 2018. The two teams then met again in Cape Town in November 2018. Through these meetings, a number of key themes relating to embedded research emerged. The first theme relates to the types of knowledge products that are developed through embedded and co-produced research arrangements. PhD theses are only one of a number of different types of knowledge products created through embedded research; embedded researchers are also producing many other kinds of knowledge products, such as policy documents, models and systems. Given the institutional homes of the embedded arrangement, the second theme revolves around the importance of power and politics (both the more intimate and everyday politics and power dynamics, and broader political mandates and political machinations), and the need for embedded researchers to be aware of, and to be able to, navigate their way through these dynamics. The third theme is about the various partnerships necessary to support the research process, both the institutional partnerships between the local government(s) and university, and the partnerships between researcher, PhD supervisor/s and municipal champions. A fourth and final theme is on process and practice, and the kinds of negotiations, methods, ethics and timeframes that are necessary for successful knowledge co-production. The knowledge transfer/exchange arrangement enables access to different kinds of knowledge, tools and methods, but also social relations. Embedded researchers can manoeuvre through city structures and say things that employees may not be able to say. Knowledge exchange also involves growing a new generation of scholars and practitioners who are able to traverse both physical and conceptual spaces, as well as produce knowledge in different registers (for example policy briefs, academic articles, models and so on).

Food

While some elements of the food work have involved comparative research across different cities around specific issues, the main overarching comparative activity has been focused on bringing together researchers involved in the different food projects to share their methods and findings, and to focus on understanding the very different approaches to food used by different researchers.

Different value perspectives on food systems inform how researchers, activists and policy makers engage in remedial actions pertaining to the food system. Four key positionalities were identified in Mistra Urban Futures' food work: a resource focus; a green focus; a food justice focus; and a scale focus. As part of the collaboration process in this project, these binaries or food system positionalities were constructed as a tool or methodological instrument to expose positions that are often assumed to be universal. These are deliberate frames or categorisations intended to make specific positions clear. The categorisations are certainly open to debate and contestation, and often overlap in practice. The areas of overlap offer clues as to where opportunities for collaboration and innovation lie. The food system positions detailed here are explained as discrete positions, but overlap and even compromise may be evident in reality.

The resource focus challenges the dominance of the so-called industrial food system (Frison and IPES-Food, 2016), holding a broader sustainability ethic. The green focus spans the food system but holds a distinct consumer focus, with a value-driven approach focused on restructuring the system, aligned with green aspirations (Friedmann, 2005; WBCSD, 2009). The food justice focus includes the food sovereignty movement (predominantly production-focused) (Patel, 2007), and other predominantly consumer-focused groupings and issue areas such as food safety, food health and food quality. A strong political line associated with justice and cultural recognition is evident. The scale-focused group is diverse. This group's key political project is one of community (broadly defined), with a distinct focus on place, or scale, and the space of flows (Soja, 2000). One of the key organising principles within this grouping is that of embeddedness or the 're-placement of food within its social, cultural, economic, geographical and environmental contexts' (Goodman and Goodman, 2009: 2; see also Feenstra, 2002). The focus is on areas such as food miles (NRDC, 2007), and ecological footprinting (Collins and Fairchild, 2007) and food production at the urban scale (Donald et al, 2010). Here focal areas include food democracy, engagement in food policy structures and local and regional food governance interventions. The connection between governance, flows and embeddedness enables new and novel ways of imagining how food systems are governed. Emerging work specific to city region food systems (Blay-Palmer et al, 2015; Vorley and Lançon, 2016; Olsson, 2018; Kotze et al, 2019) and wider urban metabolisms (Bell and Cerulli, 2012) are components of this perspective.

Diverse food system researchers and governance actors engage in food system challenges differently. For this project, framing different value positions, politics, needs and even food systems understandings was deemed an essential part of a wider interdisciplinary project on urban food system change. Practice and engagement in alternative food governance and food systems is not a process in which consensus and agreement usually exist. When viewed as a collective project, the different positions and foci offer insights into different food system processes active in the different cities. While views may differ from one city actor to another, informed largely by their own values and other factors, the different areas of focus within the different city projects offered insights into positions, priorities and even values (see Haysom et al, 2019, for an in-depth account of these framings).

Detailing these different value positions is useful for three reasons. First, it helps to identify key positions held by different researchers, and second, it enables recognition of certain non-negotiable areas or issues that participants are not willing to surrender, or where context drives such a need. Finally and perhaps most importantly, when read as a collection of responses, all focusing on the same objective – that of food system transformation – it shows how all actors, despite holding different ideological positions, are in fact working towards a common goal, rather than opposite goals. This recognition is useful because while highlighting ideological positions, it has the potential to start discussions about where the middle ground may lie, and where opportunities for compromise may sit.

This poses an important set of questions for collaborative research. How do different city researchers reconcile major global challenges and is agreement necessary? Where there is considerable food poverty in one area, is it appropriate to call for responses that originate from more middle-class settings? The answer is obviously not. However, both views have relevance and both are essential considerations. The objective, even responsibility, of a nested researcher in a particular context is to prioritise according to the urgency of need in that specific city.

For transdisciplinary and trans-contextual research into food system challenges, consensus is argued here to be a false hope, a form of co-option that dilutes deep and meaningful engagement. Finding ways to unearth and give life to difference and vastly different world views, particularly in the case of food system research where value positions are strongly held and contradictory views often disregarded, is an essential part of comparative research.

Transport

The Transport and Sustainable Urban Development project is based on the ongoing transport research at GOLIP, KLIP and CTLIP (see Cooke et al, 2019). In the process of developing the comparative project, the group members focused on getting to know one another through co-creation workshops and sessions in Kisumu, Gothenburg and Cape Town. The aim was to bring researchers and practitioners from each platform to commonly identify aim, purpose and research questions for the comparative work. In the process of identifying the research questions and main objectives of the project, a set of activities was planned. A number of workshops and site visits were held in Gothenburg, Kisumu and Cape Town between 2017 and 2019.

In the first phase of the project (2016–17), the nature of this collaboration was very unclear. There was much uncertainty about who was to be involved, and about the objectives and leadership of the project. Another challenge was to identify common objectives. The project moved from an idea phase to a framing and reframing phase in 2017–18, and then to an implementation phase in 2018–19 (see Figure 4.1).

A power dynamic appeared when attempting to identify the main objective and research questions for the comparative work. At the beginning of the project, there was an attempt to apply co-production planning methods developed in the global North to the global South. It soon became clear that there were complex issues that the group had not taken into consideration when setting up the project. For example, in Cape Town the methods of co-production planning were not transferable to the city government due to the disparity

Figure 4.1: Timeline of the Transport and Sustainable Urban Development comparative project

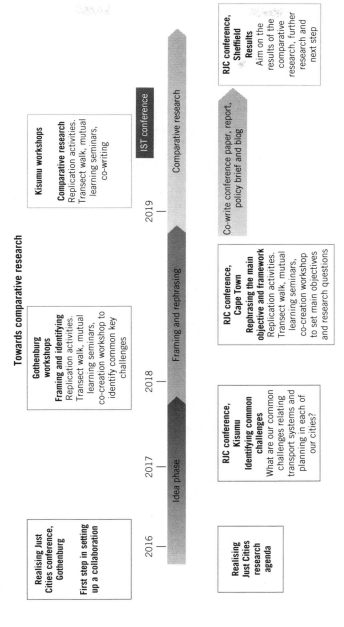

of power relations within the City of Cape Town, making it impossible to plan with participatory planning methods, and running the risk of using co-production as a way to rubber-stamp existing plans. Vanessa Watson (2014) points out that there is a need for awareness of the complexities surrounding different contexts that are often taken for granted when trying to apply methods that are developed in the global North to the global South. The idea that methods are applicable regardless of context is a simplification of reality. In retrospect, the project would have benefitted by starting the comparative work by deepening the understanding of the local complexities of each case/city and reflecting more about the power dynamics between the global North and global South, thus increasing the awareness within the group.

At the first workshops, the overall objective of the project was agreed (to undertake a comparative analysis of pursuing transport justice and its role in realising just cities) and a set of research questions was formulated:

- What are the different roles of transport across the different contexts and geographical scales?
- How does each case represent the state of transport justice discourse in each city?
- Which social justice issues are addressed in the different contexts?
- What is the equity proposition of each proposed intervention?

The comparative analysis is based on three transport interventions in each of the cities: Landvetter Södra in Gothenburg, Blue Downs Rail Link in Cape Town and the Standard Gauge Railway in Kisumu.

The replication process was developed continually. The main part of 2018 was set aside to identity main objective and research questions, in order to be able to set up comparative research. Even though the project team did not have in mind

Table 4.1: Research foci in the respective cities in the Transport and Sustainable Urban Development comparative project

Replicated activities	*Standard Gauge Railway*, Kisumu	*Blue Downs Rail Link*, Cape Town	*Landvetter Södra*, Gothenburg
Learning process of each case	Site visit to old and new stations in Kisumu	Site visit to Maitland, in-depth presentation of Blue Downs Rail Link	Site visit to Mölnlycke with in-depth presentation of Landvetter Södra
Co-creation process	Scenario workshop around the old station plus multi-criteria analysis	Walk-and-talk tour in Maitland	Walk-and-talk tour in Mölnlycke
Knowledge seminars	Internal seminar	Internal seminar	Internal seminar
Stakeholder focus groups	Focus group in Kisumu, March 2019	Focus group in Cape Town, April 2019	Focus group in Landvetter, April 2019

a specific idea of replication, there were still components that were replicated at each activity (see Table 4.1).

For each of the activities, a local team was assigned to plan for content and sessions based on local knowledge and understanding. Each team drew up a programme, co-organised with the comparative project leader. The structure of the programme was similar for each activity, with site visits, co-creative planning methods, internal knowledge seminars and stakeholder focus groups. Each activity needed to be adapted to its local context. The first workshops focused on bringing the team together, whereas the later workshops focused on setting up a project plan and conducting actual research. The stakeholder focus groups aimed to capture different perspectives of the role of transport interventions in realising just cities in each location, and what that meant in terms of the process of transitioning to a more sustainable future.

A number of outputs were planned, including a report, a paper, conference presentations, blogs and a policy brief. The outputs will provide a global North–South comparative perspective on the transition pathways that are needed in order to achieve transport justice, and will raise the question of accessibility and transport justice within the research field of sustainable transitions.

Conclusion

This chapter has discussed three comparative projects that were all, at least partially, created through the replication and adaptation of research across the Mistra Urban Futures cities. The key findings are that replication of the project work occurred in different ways across projects and across cities; that, while thematic focus and broad objectives across the cities were similar, the approaches and methods often differed considerably; and, as a result, that the approaches to comparative research also differed considerably. In addition, our experiences in developing the comparative projects have shown the importance of interactive processes for team members (who came from different disciplinary backgrounds and different places and had different perspectives) to explore ideas and identify common objectives and research questions.

As discussed, the replication of the project work across the Mistra Urban Futures cities occurred in very different ways. Quantitative research, such as the food security household surveys in the Consuming Urban Poverty project, was replicated in a fairly rigid way, but with some changes to allow for different terminology in different places. Qualitative research was replicated in a more flexible way; for example, the Transport and Sustainable Urban Development project used the same questions and methods in the three case-study projects, but adapted the process to fit the local contexts (and the nature of the projects studied). Context-specific social development interventions, such as the local government–university knowledge exchange programme in Cape Town, was replicated in an even more flexible way ('emulate' may be a more appropriate term), having the same objectives, but manifesting in quite a different way in Skåne, due to the very different context. Due to the adaptation of methods and approaches to fit local contexts and/or the different methods and approaches favoured by different teams and team members, projects on a similar theme often looked very different in different places. This was particularly evident in the food work, where a range of approaches were followed, with a notable split between a focus on localised food systems in the global North and urban food security in the global South.

As a result of the different ways in which project work was replicated and adapted, and the diversity of methods and approaches that were therefore often adopted in different cities, a variety of comparative research methods had to be followed. The Transport and Sustainable Urban Development project is the closest to a conventional comparative research project, in that it involved looking at three broadly comparable cases in the three cities. The project was largely based on the Urban Station Communities project, which had already planned to involve replication of activities from Gothenburg to Kisumu. A broadly comparable case study in Cape Town was then chosen, and the project team and joint workshops undertook more or less the same exercises for each case study (although adapted for local context), thus forming a basis for the comparative work.

The knowledge exchange comparative project also involved joint workshops where the project teams analysed the two cases – the embedded researchers in Cape Town and the municipal PhDs in Skåne. Here, however, the replication had been much more flexible, with only the broad objective being replicated and the details being very different (the Cape Town approach involved researchers moving from the university to local government, while in Skåne it was technically the other way round). In a sense, this comparative project is testing two different approaches that emerged out of two different contexts, with valuable lessons for each case that can be learned from the other.

As the Transport and Sustainable Urban Development project showed, when conducting comparative research between different cities from both the global South and North there is a need to set up an initial process to explore and define the purpose of the collaboration. As all the projects involved diverse teams with people from a range of disciplinary backgrounds and perspectives, it was crucial to bring people together in interactive processes to agree on the overall objective and detailed research questions and methods of the comparative research projects. The first part of the comparative agenda, the idea phase, can be time-consuming and complex in itself. During this period, there is a need for learning and reflection about the different local context as well as about global South–North power dynamics and the possibilities for collaboration. The second phase can be termed framing and rephrasing, during which the team conducts a series of activities (such as workshops, seminars and so on) in order to try to identify main objectives and research questions. By the end of this phase, the group should have set up a common project plan. The third phase is the comparative research phase, during which actual research is conducted. This can then be followed by subsequent phases focused on evaluation and dissemination.

Through replicating and adapting methods and objectives across cities, we were able fairly quickly to assemble comparative research projects that explored substantive and process issues relating to making cities more just and sustainable. Although working across the global North and global South highlighted power dynamics and differences in perspectives, this is essential in order to better understand how context can determine what the opportunities for, and constraints to, change in particular places are.

References

Abu-Lughod, J. (2007) 'The challenge of comparative case studies', *City*, 11(3): 399–404. doi: 10.1080/13604810701669140

Amir, Y. and Sharon, I. (1990) 'Replication research: a "must" for the scientific advancement of psychology', *Social Behavior and Personality*, 5(4): 51–69.

Anderson, P.M.L., Brown-Luthango, M., Cartwright, A., Farouk, I. and Smit, W. (2013) 'Brokering communities of knowledge and practice: reflections on the African Centre for Cities' CityLab programme', *Cities*, 32: 1–10. doi: 10.5751/ES-05076-170423

Battersby, J. and Watson, V. (eds) (2018) *Urban Food Systems Governance and Poverty in African Cities*, London: Routledge.

Begley, C.G. and Ioannidis, J.P. (2015) 'Reproducibility in science: improving the standard for basic and preclinical research', *Circulation Research*, 116(1): 116–26. doi: 10.1161/CIRCRESAHA.114.303819

Bell, S. and Cerulli, C. (2012) 'Emerging community food production and pathways for urban landscape transitions', *Emergence: Complexity & Organization,* 14(1): 31–44.

Blay-Palmer, A., Renting, H. and Dubbeling, M. (2015) *City-Region Food Systems: A Literature Review*, Leusden: RUAF Foundation. Available from: www.ruaf.org/sites/default/files/City%20Region%20Food%20Systems%20literature%20review.pdf

Collins, A. and Fairchild, R. (2007) 'Sustainable food consumption at a sub-national level: an ecological footprint', *Journal of Environmental Policy & Planning,* 9(1): 5–30. doi: 10.1080/15239080701254875

Cooke, S., Durakovic, E., Onyango, G.M., Simon, D., Singh, K., Gustafsson, A., Ranhagen, U., Lejdebro, M. and Davies, C. (2019) *Applying a Multi-Level Perspective to Examine the Potential Transition to an Accessibility-Based Approach to Transport Planning: Insights from Cities in Sweden, Kenya and South Africa*, Mistra Urban Futures. Available from: www.mistraurbanfutures.org/sites/mistraurbanfutures.org/files/190603_ist_2019_transition_to_accessibility-based_planning.pdf

Culwick, C., Washbourne, C., Anderson, P., Cartwright, A., Patel, Z. and Smit, W. (2019) 'CityLab reflections and evolutions: nurturing knowledge and learning for urban sustainability through co-production experimentation', *Current Opinion in Environmental Sustainability*, 39: 9–16. doi: 10.1016/j.cosust.2019.05.008

Donald, B., Gertler, M., Gray, M. and Lobao, L. (2010) 'Re-regionalizing the food system?', *Cambridge Journal of Regions, Economy and Society*, 3(2): 171–5. doi: 10.1093/cjres/rsq020

Dymitrow, M. and Brauer, R. (2018) 'Meaningful yet useless? Factors behind the retention of questionable concepts in human geography', *Geografiska Annaler: Series B, Human Geography*, 100(3): 195–219. doi: 10.1080/04353684.2017.1419071

Feenstra, G. (2002) 'Creating space for sustainable food systems: lessons from the field', *Agriculture and Human Values*, 19(2): 99–106.

Friedmann, H. (2005) 'From colonialism to green capitalism: social movements and the emergence of food regimes', in F. Buttel, and P. McMichael (eds) *New Directions in the Sociology of Global Development*, Oxford: Elsevier, pp 227–64.

Frison, E.A. and IPES-Food (2016) *From Uniformity to Diversity: A Paradigm Shift from Industrial Agriculture to Diversified Agroecological Systems*, Louvain-la-Neuve: IPES.

Goodman, D. and Goodman, M. (2009) 'Alternative food networks', in R. Kitchen and N. Thrift (eds) *International Encyclopedia of Human Geography, Volume 8*, Oxford: Elsevier.

Haysom, G., Olsson, E.G.A., Dymitrow, M., Opiyo, P., Taylor Buck, N., Oloko, M., Spring, C., Fermskog, K., Ingelhag, K., Kotze. S. and Agong, S.G. (2019) 'Food systems sustainability: an examination of different viewpoints on food system change', *Sustainability*, 11(12): 3337. doi: 10.3390/su11123337

Kotze, S., Dymitrow, M. and Ingelhag, K. (2019) 'Can a city feed itself? Innovations in City–Region Food Systems from a Swedish perspective', Paper presented at the 4th Global Food Security, Food Safety & Sustainability Conference, Montreal, Canada, 10–11 May.

Miszczak, S.M. and Patel, Z. (2018) 'The role of engaged scholarship and co-production to address urban challenges: a case study of the Cape Town Knowledge Transfer Programme', *South African Geographical Journal*, 100(2): 233–48. doi: 10.1080/03736245.2017.1409649

Moonesinghe, R., Khoury, M.J. and Janssens, A.C.J.W. (2007) 'Most published research findings are false – but a little replication goes a long way', *PLOS Medicine*, 4(2): e28. doi: 10.1371/journal.pmed.0040028

NRDC (Natural Resources Defence Council) (2007) *Food Miles: Health Facts*, New York, NY: NRDC.

Olsson, E.G.A. (2018) 'Urban food systems as vehicles for sustainability transitions', *Bulletin of Geography: Socio-Economic Series*, 40: 133–44. doi: 10.2478/bog-2018-0019

Opiyo, P. and Agong, S. (2018) *Food Security in Kisumu: A Call for Greater Engagement in the Urban Food System*, Consuming Urban Poverty Policy Brief No. 1, Cape Town: African Centre for Cities, University of Cape Town.

Opiyo, P., Obange, N., Ogindo, H. and Wagah, G. (2018a) *The Characteristics, Extent and Drivers of Urban Food Poverty in Kisumu, Kenya*, Consuming Urban Poverty Project Working Paper No. 4, Cape Town: African Centre for Cities, University of Cape Town.

Opiyo, P., Ogindo, H. and Otiende, F. (2018b) *Characteristics of the Urban Food System in Kisumu, Kenya*, Consuming Urban Poverty Project Working Paper No. 5, Cape Town: African Centre for Cities, University of Cape Town.

Pashler, H. and Wagenmakers, E.J. (2012) 'Editors' introduction to the special section on replicability in psychological science: a crisis of confidence?', *Perspectives on Psychological Science*, 7(6): 528–30. doi: 10.1177/1745691612465253

Patel, R. (2007) *Stuffed and Starved*, New York, NY: Melville House.

Ranhagen, U., Dahlstrand, A. and Ramstedt (2017) *Co-Creation in Urban Station Communities*, Gothenburg: Mistra Urban Futures. Available from: www.mistraurbanfutures.org/en/publication/co-creation-urban-station-communities

Repko, A.F. and Szostak, R. (2016) *Interdisciplinary Research: Process and Theory* (3rd edn), Los Angeles, CA: Sage Publications.

Schooler, J.W. (2014) 'Metascience could rescue the "replication crisis"', *Nature*, 515(7525): 9. doi: 10.1038/515009a

Scott, D., Davies, H. and New, M. (eds) (2019) *Mainstreaming Climate Change in Urban Development: Lessons from Cape Town*, Cape Town: University of Cape Town Press.

Simons, D.J. (2014) 'The value of direct replication', *Perspectives on Psychological Science,* 9(1), 76–80.

Smit, W., Lawhon, M. and Patel, Z. (2015) 'Co-producing knowledge for whom, and to what end? Reflections from the African Centre for Cities in Cape Town', in M. Polk (ed) *Co-Producing Knowledge for Sustainable Cities: Joining Forces for Change*, Abingdon: Routledge, pp 47–69.

Smith, N. (2017) 'Why "statistical significance" is often insignificant', *Bloomberg*, 2 November.

Soja, E. (2000) *Postmetropolis: Critical Studies of City Region*s, Oxford: Blackwell.

Vorley, B. and Lançon, F. (2016) *Food Consumption, Urbanisation and Rural Transformation: The Trade Dimensions*, London: International Institute for Environment and Development.

Watson, V. (2014) 'Co-production and collaboration in planning – the difference', *Planning Theory & Practice*, 15(1): 62–76. doi: 10.1080/14649357.2013.866266

WBCSD (World Business Council for Sustainable Development) (2009) *Agricultural Ecosystems: Facts and Trends*, Geneva: WBCSD.

FIVE

Clustering and assemblage building

Henrietta Palmer, Erica Righard and Nils Björling, with Eva Maria Jernsand, Helena Kraff and Lillian Omondi

'As if entering into a shared space from different doors – but without a floor to walk upon.'
Workshop meeting, Cape Town, 2018

Introduction

Everyone with an interest in the urban will consciously or unconsciously compare earlier experiences of other urban environments with what is experienced at hand; they will be 'thinking (cities) through elsewhere' (Robinson, 2015: 195). It is therefore difficult to imagine any other situation where such comparative activities play out more distinctively than in urban situations induced by migration and other forms of mobility. Who is ever better set to do urban comparison than migrants constantly reminded of places left behind and trying to make sense of places of arrival? Therefore, migration is ultimately connected to comparative urbanism in what Jacobs calls 'an everyday comparison' (Jacobs, 2012: 910).

This chapter describes comparative knowledge production by way of bringing together already existing research financed by other means and local development projects within a defined area of research and intervention. The projects were all dealing with migration but based in different urban contexts, and they were brought together in a systematic way we call clustering. This methodology was developed through a joint venture of comparative knowledge production involving researchers, practitioners and civil society actors at the Local Interactive Platforms (LIPs) in Gothenburg (GOLIP), Skåne (SKLIP) and Kisumu (KLIP). Based within the Mistra Urban Futures agenda for comparative research and its understanding of co-produced transdisciplinary research (as discussed in Chapters One and Two), this was a natural starting point. The project originally stemmed from a need to better understand international migration, and in particular refugee reception and integration, as this developed in Gothenburg and Malmö following the so-called refugee crisis in 2015. It was later reframed to include the situation of rural–urban migration in Kisumu and research at the intersection of inclusive tourism, urban multiculturalism and sustainable development in, among other places, Malmö, Gothenburg and Kisumu. As the work proceeded, it became clear that, at the urban level, migration and its consequences have similarities across varying societal contexts and that learning exchanges are valid.

Clustering represents a method for comparison and knowledge production across discrete research and development projects within a joint field or theme, but based in dissimilar societal contexts. Inspired by assemblage theory, as originally conceptualised by Gilles Deleuze and Felix Guattari (1987) and later developed and brought into the field of design and design thinking by Manuel DeLanda (2006), relevant key questions were identified to guide the comparative work. This approach enabled participants to exchange and discuss experiences, build new knowledges and elaborate potentials across projects and localities without full understanding of the often very different background, context and dynamic of each project. The contribution of the chapter lies primarily in its presentation of a methodology for knowledge exchange and building in a transdisciplinary and translocal setting, without a budget to fund a rigorous and systematic comparison on the empirical level.

The chapter first describes how this work proceeded over time; it outlines how the comparative method of clustering evolved from the first initiative to the consolidated framework resulting from the working process. The second section elaborates on clustering as a comparative method in a more general way, including positioning it in relevant theoretical debates. It then critically revisits the method of clustering, its benefits and challenges, and describes how some of the challenges were overcome. The final section of the chapter discusses how clustering as a comparative method can contribute to the overall aim of Mistra Urban Futures, namely that of Realising Just Cities.

Setting the scene: a chronology

The implementation of this comparative project was shaped by how it came about and the conditions under which it worked. We argue that our method is a case of clustering, but in fact it resembles much of a what we often think of as a research network, that is a gathering of researchers working on a common theme, but often from different disciplinary perspectives, universities or countries, for instance, usually with a limited budget for running costs related to network meetings but not research activities per se. The reason why we insist on this not being just a research network is the more systematic method derived from design theory we applied in our comparative work and which, we argue, contributed added value to each of the projects involved. This section describes how the clustering developed over time as new partners were involved in a stepwise manner, and how the comparative themes, discussed as 'entry points' in the section on theorising clustering, were identified in conjunction with this.

Defining the theme: migration and urban development

The comparative project was broadly entitled Migration and Urban Development and was set to focus on urban and regional development in relation to migration, including persons of varying migration backgrounds, legal statuses and citizenship. Through the opportunity to conduct comparative studies across Mistra Urban Futures' LIPs, the aim was to identify and understand the challenges and opportunities that migration presents in relation to sustainable urban development. Migration in the different urban settings involved various forms of migration, and a theoretical approach was developed for the comparative research that merged internal migration, primarily related to urbanisation processes, with international migration into a common framework. As international and internal migration are often separated by disciplinary boundaries, namely those of migration studies and urban studies, with this propositional project came an opportunity to contribute to a research direction integrating the two into one.

The project aimed at developing a multifaceted body of research for the consolidation and expansion of this integrated approach to migration and urban development, to further contribute as a compelling pilot for Mistra Urban Futures' strategic planning beyond 2020. It also set out to build knowledge alliances among academics, civil servants and civil society actors, enabling them to be well informed about each other's respective fields of knowledge, expertise and experiences, thus providing a grounding for future collaborations within this field of knowledge building.

Since the project inauguration by the Gothenburg and Skåne platforms in early 2017, the project has gone through different stages, formats of knowledge production, and actors' constellations and engagement. Openness and inclusiveness were conscious approaches to avoid getting stuck in the national or local perspectives preconceived by the initiators, but rather to be influenced by new project partners. However, as discussed later in this chapter, this 'openness' also involved disruptions of the working process; hence, a balance of openness and closedness is needed when staging this kind of inquiry. Within the approach, the concept of clustering became relevant, as the aligning projects were quite different from one another and not immediately comparable across local or national contexts. As a methodology, clustering was initially vague and did not offer any immediate guidance. Hence, to explore clustering as a methodology and to understand its potential for comparative knowledge building became a meta-goal of this project, beyond the objectives of the individual projects.

As this short chronology shows, the project itself emerged through different concerns and was shaped through the ongoing conceptualisation of clustering. It also shows how the method of clustering was fleshed out to become more instructive for the comparative research.

The initial step: commonalities of international and internal migration

A first scanning of interest in the field took place in Gothenburg in 2017 among around 30 practitioners from the public and civil sector from Malmö and Gothenburg, together with researchers from the Chalmers University of Technology, University of Gothenburg and Malmö University. The discussion was organised along three sub-themes. For the continued work at GOLIP, these themes remained productive; they were merged into one, forming the basis of the first GOLIP-funded research project related to migration.[1]

As the first initiative was taken by two Swedish LIPs, the research on migration and urban development was not initially engaged in a cross-national comparison. A first international meeting for a possible comparative project was staged at the Mistra Urban Futures annual conference in Kisumu in November 2017. It was decided then to not promote the themes that had framed the project up to this point, as they were biased towards the Swedish aftermaths of the comparatively large influx of asylum seekers from Syria and other war-torn countries in late 2015, and not necessarily relevant to the LIPs in other countries. Taking into consideration the varying situations of migration in the different urban contexts, project proposals were invited from other Mistra Urban Futures LIPs to enter into the comparative inquiry of migration and urban development. The workshop in Kisumu engaged participants interested in intersections of urban and migration issues that could form comparative approaches relevant to all platforms. The most important result was the notion of translocality, which allowed for understandings of both international migration and internal rural-to-urban migration, and hence resonated for all participants and their different experiences and research interests. This conceptual definition also became the first stepping stone for further development of the comparative methodological strategy.

Consolidation: four transformative themes

A second international workshop, in early 2018 in Malmö, involved ongoing research and development initiatives (not only research and development *interests* this time) related to migration and urban development. The initiatives had their base within the Mistra Urban Futures LIPs or existed in the 'vicinity' of the platforms. Fourteen participants, from both academia and practice, presented their ongoing research in six separate projects. The workshop was dominated by participants from the Gothenburg and Malmö platforms, with only one researcher and one practitioner from outside Sweden, namely Kisumu. A researcher from the University of Sheffield was connected via Skype.

The workshop was organised into a series of short presentations of the different research and development initiatives. In the discussions and reflections on the presentations, and what migration meant to each project constellation, four cross-cutting and 'transformative' themes were identified: territories, practices, collaborations and languages. These themes were cross-cutting in the sense that they had relevance across all platforms and projects. What happened at this meeting was a first consolidation of comparative knowledge building as a joint enterprise. Even though some of the individual projects later decided to opt out from this comparative work, mainly due to lack of time and financial resources, the group started to develop innovative research directions and to plan for joint outputs. What previously had been merely a common interest in the topic of migration and urban development now served to engage the participants in joint project activities, which, among other things, resulted in a successful research bid in mid-2018 for a large project entitled Tourism in Multicultural Societies, including researchers from the universities in Gothenburg, Malmö and Kisumu. It can be argued that, at this point, the comparative project developed from being merely a topic-based network, to become an 'alliance of committedness' to both the content of comparative work and to the method of doing this work. A key reason for this to develop, we argue, was the emergence of the cross-cutting themes that created a sense of co-ownership in terms of a joint framework, which in turn generated new perspectives within the individual research projects. Hence, clustering was developed into a two-fold methodology, first, as a knowledge alliance across disciplinary and organisational boundaries, asking for a particular structure, protocols, documentation and practice, and, second, as content-oriented comparative work driven by defined transformative themes.

Advancement: process as outcome

Beyond a number of less formal meetings taking place between some of the individual participants whenever an opportunity emerged, the next prepared workshop was planned in conjunction with the Mistra Urban Futures annual conference in Cape Town in November 2018. The meeting was staged as an inquiry into the research and local development projects involved, assisted by the now defined method of comparison. The challenges and risks of working through a knowledge alliance were considered, with new participants from practice and academia joining in for the first time. With early results from the four transformative themes, the researchers and practitioners were able to reflect on and debate whether or not these had been productive in their individual projects.

With input from design-based research, a suggestion for a conceptualisation of clustering was made to understand clustering through assemblage theory, and the concept of 'composition'. In her taxonomy of urban comparison, Jennifer Robinson suggests composing comparisons as a distinguishable mood of comparing, as 'design[ing] bespoke projects grounded in shared features' (2015: 196) rather than in a comparison of similarities or differences. This compositional approach resembles that of assemblage. Although not everyone in the group was familiar with assemblage theory or such an approach, it was a stimulating argument that made everyone curious enough to want to explore it further. Against this background, initiators could discern how to create a comparative narrative of a number of discrete research projects (at this point four projects), coming from different contexts and based in varying epistemological assumptions. The sensation of overview also relaxed some of the anxieties and doubts regarding whether it was worthwhile engaging in a knowledge alliance of this kind. It is essential to raise these concerns, since allocated time and funding do set out important preconditions for collaborative and co-produced engagements, and indeed individual participants were grappling with the inadequacy of these. But, importantly, in our experience, clarity in the process design, a common understanding and the emergence of new perspectives can, at least partly, substitute for this lack. This was pointed out by the participants who were supportive of further consolidation and of the method development.

In the following knowledge alliance session, in Gothenburg in March 2019, work continued determinedly on deepening the transformative themes, and participants were asked to present their work from an inquiry into these themes. At this point, five projects were involved. Three had been involved from the initial phase, while two joined subsequently. In addition to the two research projects already mentioned, one addressed the organisation of labour market integration from the perspective of a non-governmental organisation (GOLIP), one was about housing, language training, and labour market integration among asylum seekers and newly arrived refugees (SKLIP), and one concerned the structure and role of social networks of rural migrants arriving in urban areas (KLIP). A main issue raised in the workshop concerned to what extent the four themes were guiding the analytical work and knowledge production in the individual projects, and to what extent they were addressing how the transdisciplinary co-production that each project was engaged with separately was accomplished. Clearly, co-produced transdisciplinary research is central to the ethos of Mistra Urban Futures and the preconditions for such research approaches, as discussed in Chapter Two. Of relevance here is that the knowledge alliances at hand bore features that resonated with our themes, namely the crossing of boundaries, including boundaries of territories, practices and languages. In this double-sighted view, the themes enabled us to discuss the transformative themes as, on the one hand, determining the characteristic of the knowledge alliance itself, and, on the other hand, as analytical lenses for the comparative knowledge production. The conclusion reached was that it is relevant to consider both the 'what' and the 'how' of the transdisciplinary and comparative co-production of knowledge. From a detailed examination of the project presentations, comments were organised to address the various forms of 'what' and 'how', and their performative outcomes. These two distinctions speak to the transformative properties of the themes, describing them both in terms of a process of transformation and as the outcomes of such.

Besides these emerging definitions, two important findings and conclusions advanced our method. The first one was to eliminate the theme of transformative collaboration, as this could be collapsed into transformative practices, thus avoiding confusion with the overall collaborative research approach of transdisciplinary co-production. The second one was that in combining process and outcomes, the 'how' and 'what' of the analytical work, each thematic lens became redefined through these combined properties. The transformative territories, as identified in the Kisumu workshop, would now be described as 'translocality', the transformative practices as 'trans-sectionality', and the transformative language as 'trans-language' (see the next section). With these new findings, clustering as a productive method had the potential to reach beyond mere network capacities. While this sequential development was dependent on an embedded dynamic and was unintentional, we shall now revisit it with a systematic and more theoretical gaze.

Theorising clustering

Clustering, as applied in this comparative project, is given a double meaning and form. The first form is clustering of project participants into a knowledge alliance, and the second is a clustering of substantive projects as a composition or an assemblage building. The assemblage building was initially structured by four, later reduced to three, transformative themes. These became our entry points into a common construction of extracts from our different references and experiences. The assemblage building was thereby composed around a set of key questions/themes, rather than being defined by a set of cases. Here we outline and discuss what knowledge alliance, assemblage building and entry points as methodological concepts carry in terms of practical and critical imaginative capacities.

Knowledge alliances

The clustering of project participants into knowledge alliances diverged from collaborative settings where differences or similarities of selected cases are compared by teams across different contexts. It also differed from network meetings focused on specific thematic fields, which mainly aim at gathering knowledge and expertise to an available and accessible setting. By contrast, in this particular project, being transdisciplinary and comparative, the participants came from both academia and practice, hence not only bearing with them different knowledges, but also mandates, forms of legitimacy and capacities for interaction, which also clearly set different preconditions compared with most research networks. Andreas Novy and colleagues (2014: 433) define knowledge alliances as partnerships in which members '… share, produce and diffuse knowledge and build bridges between fragmented entities …'. This was very evident in our case and, from our experience, knowledge alliances gain from a common thematic structure beyond the topic of research, and by a collective mindedness to develop a particular field of inquiry. In doing so, a certain frequency of meetings is required, as well as a certain consistency of group participants in order to not get stuck in the mode of continuous repetition or starting over when concepts are tested and reflected on as they are being developed. Moreover, protocols are needed for the introduction of new persons when a participant cannot participate any longer due to changed circumstances. Documentation of the working process is essential, also for the knowledge alliance to develop beyond the designated meetings. These descriptions and reflections should be shared continually to generate experiences of productive situations and a readiness for the comparative work when it is about to take place. This documentation also spurs iterations beyond the main process, as participants through the reflective work find reasons to engage with each other in other, albeit related, areas and contexts.

In part, this approach diverges from transdisciplinary co-production as elaborated by Mistra Urban Futures. One divergence is found at the moment of inauguration. In this view, the project members should preferably define the problem jointly and invite participants who can contribute and add further knowledge that expands the kind of knowledge already existent within the group. Contrastingly, in this case, the knowledge alliance was initiated by a small group without a specific problem definition and came to assemble a number of projects related to a broader field of inquiry instead of a specified research problem. However, the openness of the process, the expansion of the project group, the iterations and the reflexivity share properties with a process of transdisciplinary co-production.

Assemblage building

The critique of 'best practices' has relevance here, as it can function to position comparative urbanism as part of a developmentalism agenda (Robinson, 2011). A replication and copying of practices from one context to another, with the ambition to solve a problem, could 'push past the target', as problems, albeit general in their impact, are often situated and solutions therefore have situated properties as well. Following on this, while learning from one context to another is inherent to any comparative endeavour, unconsciously replicating solutions that work in one context to another should be avoided, and this is central to the comparative ethos of Mistra Urban Futures (see Chapter Two). This understanding also emerged from the discussions, and reinforced the usefulness of the concept of assemblage building. Through an assemblage, we see projects as related, not individually but to the larger composition. This makes it possible to start a comparison around available information of a specific theme rather than with the full contextual knowledge of each one of the different research projects or case studies. Hence, we can discuss, transfer and develop knowledge between the projects (based in different territories, sectors and languages) without fully understanding the nuances, often embedded in the varying backgrounds, situations and disciplines that have informed and shaped the development of each one.

Colin McFarlane (2011) has identified three strands of thinking and forming of assemblage in urban theory: as a descriptive focus through which explanations emerge from a thick description; as a way to rethink agency, particularly in relation to socio-material interaction; and as critical imaginary through the composition as such. In our case, the last strand resonates well: themes emerged as a critical response to how territories, practices and languages have impact on the integration of (internal and international) migrants in different ways across different urban contexts. One could further use design thinking, whereas design-based research often uses assemblage building as a method (DeLanda, 2006; Björling, 2016), that is, trying out multiple constellations of different parts for the opening-up of new imaginaries. A comparison in this manner is then the result of both the potential of included knowledge, references and experiences and their internal and external relations (Deleuze and Guattari, 1987). Through the selection of themes and key questions, assemblage theory becomes potentially useful. At the same time as the assemblage establishes a dynamic starting point for comparison, it emphasises continual rearrangement of components and processes and thereby also has the capacity to combine ongoing transformations and changing conditions within the different contexts. According to Manuel DeLanda (2006), the productive capacity of the assemblage depends on the interplay between its individual parts of knowledge and the co-productive capacity of the whole. To understand the engaged projects as an assemblage form or composition gives a freedom also to ask new questions from the content and designed format of the assemblage. A process of interplay takes place as the assemblage in turn is transformed and reveals a common start for development of the knowledge of the group. McFarlane (2011) points out that due to the adaptability embedded in the properties of an assemblage, one might avoid using the potential of conflicts and contradictions between parts, but rather find 'lines of flight' that name the possibility of creating something new. We decided to call our emerging lines of flight entry points and designated the three remaining themes identified, namely transformative territories, transformative practices and transformative languages, as entry points for clustering of knowledge and practices.

Entry points

To contextualise this discussion, we provide a short back-tracing of the definitions of the original four themes, which were set as an outcome of the Malmö workshop.

'Transformative territories' implies a re-territorialisation of integration. Within this theme, territories are regarded as productive in terms of creating conditions for integration and further urban development, as well as products themselves of social practices related to migration and integration. 'Transformative practices' implies that alternative and/or organically developed practices could contribute to inclusion at a local level, but also be transformed by societal processes of inclusion. 'Transformative collaborations' implies that new types of collaboration are needed to address the challenges and harvest the opportunities that arise in cities' reception of international and internal migrants. It implies collaboration across sectors, silos and cities, as well as the transformation of different roles with respect to migration and urban development. 'Transformative languages' implies that language has a performative role and reflects on which language is used and how it is used when addressing migration in relation to urban development.

The last Gothenburg workshop was designated as an interrogation of these definitions. What had been the relevance of these themes for the ongoing research until this point in time? What suggestions for additional readings could be made? The propositional definition of the themes as transformative indicates a two-pathway production in each of them. This feature was clarified, meaning that the transformative capacity was described as both a process and a performative outcome. As a result of these interrogations, the four themes were redefined as three, partly since collaboration resonates in two distinct ways – in both the empirical analysis and the transdisciplinary research process as such, that is, in both the 'what' and the 'how', as discussed earlier. In addition, many of the workshop participants agreed that the empirical findings of collaborative transformations were closely connected to findings of the transformative practices. The identification of a number of empirical examples of the three remaining themes in each research project enabled critical reflection on these themes across the projects. This enabled a fruitful way of building knowledge that was place-specific and, at the same time, informed by insights from other contexts.

One further evolution regards how the entry points, through their readings, cross projects, and how, through their double productive properties, they can be redefined. The transformative territories, as had already been addressed in the Kisumu workshop, were now framed as translocality.[2] The transformative practice was redefined as trans-sectionality, and the transformative language as trans-language. These three concepts all share the notion of crossing different kinds of boundaries and of having plural and relational belongings. The first one is known and deployed in geography, anthropology and migration studies, pointing towards the situated nature of transnational networks (see, for example, Brickell and Datta, 2011) and emerging as a research field in its own right (Greiner and Sakdapolrak, 2013). The concept of transsectionality has evolved lately as a proposition to provide the framework of intersectionality with a fluidity in the definitions of identities. As intersectionality proposes a layered number of identities within each person, trans-sectionality suggests that these identities are never permanent but can change and be reconstituted (Nicole, 2014). In our case, this speaks more to (professional) 'roles' than 'identities', as we discussed them in terms of transcending different mandates in relation to practices engaged in processes of urban inclusion.

Trans-language stems from pedagogy and implies not insisting on one language only in a pedagogical situation, but allowing and stimulating the use of more languages, often the national majority language (see, for example, Canagarajah, 2011), but here it also regards languages of varying professions and academic disciplines (see also Nikulina et al, 2019). While transformative language was introduced as a theme to reflect critically on how language takes a performative role in processes of migration and urban development, the concept of trans-language opens an uncertainty that can undermine pre-set definitions in a productive way.

In the context of comparative urban discourses, Jane M. Jacobs has pointed out that finding methods that are sensitive to 'trans', such as translocal, transurban and translation, can give us important keys to the objects of comparative urbanism. She suggests that it can be exactly the transformative processes of cities that create commonalities between them. Jacobs states that as anthropology has provided us with the notion of multi-sited ethnographies through which to understand the production of global effects, it has also:

'given rise in geography to thinking through networks and assemblages, and ... for thinking beyond models of the diffusion of stable objects (policies, models of architectural form) to more open concepts of translation and transduction, in which there is a constant remaking of the world through reiterative practices.' (Jacobs, 2012: 908)

This is a compelling remark that speaks to the definition of our overall project at the intersection of urbanism and migration. At this intersection, clustering as a comparative typology has evoked three trans-concepts, which are both critical and imaginative, and possibly productive for the making of just cities.

Benefits and challenges

The learning outcomes of this project relate to the content of the comparative work, and to the conceptualisation of the comparative method. It is a shared understanding among the participants that clustering and how it evolved, both in terms of a knowledge alliance and as the building of a project assemblage, provided fruitful learning to each of the individual research projects. However, since all research projects are still ongoing, the particular impact on each individual research project is still too early to delineate. Learning outcomes relating to the comparative methodology and its conceptualisation are more distinguishable at this point. The challenges and benefits of collaborative work are well examined in the literature on participatory practices. Many of these are similar to the challenges and benefits of clustering as a process. Here we therefore do not linger on outcomes such as mutual learning and network effects (Wiek et al, 2014), but rather address other benefits and challenges possibly significant for clustering as co-produced transdisciplinary research.

Process design and group consolidation

From our experience, knowledge alliances and the method of assemblage cannot be too elusive. Someone must both lead the project and the design of the project as such. In parallel, it was acknowledged that some kind of project consolidation or institutionalisation must take place to create a certain degree of stability. Otherwise the project is trapped in a very unstable format. This institutionalisation, we argue, happens through the repetition of meetings in which participation initially is a 'soft commitment' but eventually becomes 'harder', as well as through the development of a shared understanding of the joint endeavour and its design. As time is precious for everyone involved, the design of the project has to be put in place in a transparent manner by someone who can dedicate both time and reflexive work to the project institutionalisation, as it is not realistic to expect this to happen fully in the common meetings.

For the implementation of clustering as a comparative methodology, at least in our case, it is important to stress the setting. This comparative endeavour was embedded within a long-term collaboration between LIPs within Mistra Urban Futures. This setting enabled an iterative process between, on the one hand, the development of individual projects, and on the other, a series of joint workshops, seminars and conferences, which would probably be much more challenging in other, more temporary, settings.

Another lesson learned is that although it has been essential for this project to be agile and responsive, which works well for both the knowledge alliance and for the substantive assemblage, one also needs to define the extent to which flexibility is productive. When is the time to close the group to new project members and stop elaborating on project definition and goals? When is it time to define the entry points to which comparison can be made? Consolidating too early brings the risk of excluding potentially fruitful collaborations and imaginaries, while doing so too late might actually prevent consolidation and lead to members leaving the project. There is no clear recipe for how this should happen. From our experience, this balance is contestable and delicate and needs to be discussed openly.

Uncertainty and the role of a narrative

As already described, clustering as a process is difficult to control. It depends on possible funding, possible co-engagements beyond what is set by the knowledge alliance, and the possible establishment of new projects. Together this implies that time planning and results are difficult to foresee. Even pre-set meetings can be postponed, as the collaboration is constantly looking for the fulfilment of short-term objectives, and when these are not within sight, the immediate relevance of knowledge alliance activities declines. Comparative projects with a devoted budget typically have a fixed project plan with expected outcomes. But when there is no budget, participants, processes and outcomes tend to be continually renegotiated and ever-changing. In the absence of a fixed plan, continual documentation of each developmental stage of the project becomes essential for the process to institutionalise. This is an effect of the set-up, and experiences from various 'commoning' processes witness similar urgency (Stavrides, 2016; Džokić and Neelen, 2018). Documentation needs to take on a reflective and narrative role, not only to give access to the process, design and the shared language for established projects participants as well as potential new ones, but also to set the agenda in terms of suggesting structuring concepts regulating and shaping the process forward. One such narrative is the realising of just cities. The following and final section briefly comments on how this comparative project possibly has the potential to contribute a narrative to the overall achievement of Mistra Urban Futures' comparative work.

Contribution to realising just cities

Mistra Urban Futures' aim is realising just cities. To raise the question of how a limited endeavour like this comparative project contributes to this overarching aim is, of course, as ambitious as it is necessary. Here we reflect on how, from our experiences, this comparative project has taken some small steps towards contributing to learning about migration and urban development as well as how the methodology of clustering can be further applied and possibly contribute to urban justice.

Clustering as a method for cross-city learning in globalised societies

Clustering, as developed in this comparative project, offers a method for comparison and learning across discrete projects and, in several ways, fundamentally different urban contexts. It can be implemented without large funding, but relies on existing and funded research and development projects. The defined entry points enabled exchanges and knowledge production across territorial, practice and language boundaries while remaining context-sensitive. The outcome is, on the one hand, a shared set of concepts, as described earlier, which as 'lines of flight' can be brought back to individual research projects where new theory and practice can be outlined. Through this comparative method, the knowledge production is localised, as outcomes from the comparative work are inserted back into the projects. In line with Jennifer Robinson's questions about whether we can 'promote theory cultures which are alert to their own locatedness ... and committed to the revisability of theoretical ideas' (2016: 188), this is an important point to embrace. Moreover, in this way, the approach of clustering not only takes a critical stance on 'best practices', but also offers a way forward and beyond such approaches.

While we estimate that clustering has proved a fruitful method to address comparative urban research, obviously funding for comparative work is crucial to extract a meta-narrative from a number of discrete research projects. As funding has only been available for a discursive level, much of the comparative research within this project still remains to be done. However, we consider the methodological advance made to be an important research contribution in itself and suggest it as a response to Jennifer Robinson's call for an experimental comparative urbanism across the imagination of a global North–South division (Robinson, 2011).

Ways forward

In her work on urban justice, Susan Fainstein (2013) examines three urban contexts in a comparative inquiry. Her definition of urban justice, with references to democracy, diversity and equity, responds to Nancy Fraser's definitions of justice as representation, recognition and redistribution (or participation, identities and material distribution) (Fraser, 1996, 2000). The three concepts bearing the prefix 'trans' and developed in this comparative project – translocality, trans-sectionality and trans-language – can be considered in the light of Fainstein's and Frasers's discussions. The prefix 'trans' responds to a liminal condition of being both *in between* different territories, roles/identities and languages, and *towards*, as in a process of transformation, where the outcome of such a process is not set. Here, we want to advocate an opening in discussions about realising just cities; the three concepts could function to raise new propositions for planning from pre-set and fixed positions of citizens to an acceptance of in-between positions, including, for instance, positions of belonging to multiple territories, fluid roles and agencies, and the conscious use of multiple languages as performative actions. Such a future framework calls for a reconceptualisation of what it is to belong, and how justice and just cities should be conceptualised in translocal settings.

Acknowledgements

This comparative project is based on the collaboration of civil servants and researchers from Mistra Urban Futures' local interactive platforms in Gothenburg, Kisumu and Malmö (GOLIP, KLIP and SKLIP). As writers of this chapter, we thank all the participants who have, at different stages, contributed to the development of this work: Maher Akob, Ester Barinaga, Emma Björner, Kristina Grange, Hanna Hellgren, Sanna Isemo, Maria

Hellström Reimer, Helene Holmström, Sandra Lundberg, Jennie Ström, Steven Sule, Caroline Wanjiku Kihato, Maria José Zapata Campos and Klara Öberg.

The comparative project builds on the following research projects: Organizing Integration, WP 3, based at the University of Gothenburg and funded by the Swedish Research Council for Health, Working Life and Welfare, together with GOLIP/ Mistra Urban Futures in 2017–20; Migrant Networks and Leverage, based at Maseno University and funded by KLIP/ Mistra Urban Futures, 2018–19; Governance and the Local Integration of Migrants and Europe's Refugees, based at Malmö University and funded through ERA-NET Sustainable Urban Futures under the European Union Research and Innovation Programme Horizon 2020, with funding for the Swedish part from the Swedish Research Council for Sustainable Development, Formas, in 2017–20; The Uneven Geography of Migration, based at Chalmers University of Technology and funded by GOLIP/Mistra Urban Futures in 2018–19; and *Turismens roll i multikulturella samhällen* (Tourism in Multicultural Societies), based at Malmö University and funded by Formas from 2019–22.

Notes

[1] The Uneven Geography of Migration is a research project comparing how a law about housing for newly arrived refugees, effective as of 1 March 2016, affected the recipience of migrants in three municipalities in western Sweden. Details of this and the other projects on which this comparative endeavour is based, appear in the acknowledgements on pp 109–10.

[2] The concept of translocality was also central in the keynote lecture by Caroline Wanjiku Kihato at the Mistra Urban Futures annual conference 2017. See https://youtu.be/6s78-axClNk

References

Björling, N. (2016) 'Sköra stadslandskap: planeringsmetoder för att hantera urbaniseringens rumsliga inlåsningar' (Fragile urban landscapes: planning methods to open spatial lock-ins of urbanization), Doctoral thesis, Gothenburg: Chalmers University of Technology.

Brickell, K. and Datta, A. (eds) (2011) *Translocal Geographies: Spaces, Places, and Connections*, Farnham: Ashgate.

Canagarajah, S. (2011) 'Translanguaging in the classroom: emerging issues for research and pedagogy', *Applied Linguistics Review*, 2(1): 1-28.

DeLanda, M. (2006) *A New Philosophy of Society: Assemblage Theory and Social Complexity*, New York, NY: Continuum International Publishing Group.

Deleuze, G. and Guattari, F. (1987) *A Thousand Plateaus: Capitalism and Schiozophrenia*, Minneapolis, MN: University of Minnesota Press.

Džokić, A. and Neelen, M. (2018) *Upscaling, Training, Commoning: Constructing a Future That is Yet to be*, Berlin: Jovis.

Fainstein, S. (2013) 'The just city', *International Journal of Urban Sciences*, 18(1): 1–18. doi: 10.1080/ 12265934.2013.834643

Fraser, N. (1996) 'Social justice in the age of identity politics: redistribution, recognition and participation', Tanner Lectures on Human Values, Stanford University, 30 April –2 May, 1996.

Fraser, N. (2000) 'Rethinking recognition', *New Left Review*, May–June, 2000(3): 107–20.

Greiner, C. and Sakdapolrak, P. (2013) 'Translocality: concepts, applications and emerging research perspectives', *Geography Compass*, 7/5: 373–84. doi:10.1111/gec3.12048

Jacobs, J.M. (2012) 'Commentary: comparing comparative urbanisms', *Urban Geography*, 33(6): 904–914. doi: 10.2747/ 0272-3638.33.6.904

McFarlane, C. (2011) 'Assemblage and critical urbanism', *City*, 15(2): 204–24. doi: 10.1080/13604813.2011.568715

Nicole, K. (2014) 'Trans-forming identities: integrating intersectionality and trans-sectionality', *iintrospectivescience* [Blog]. Available from: https://iintrospectivescience.wordpress.com/2014/04/01/trans-forming-identities-integrating-intersectionality-and-trans-sectionality [Accessed 23 September 2019].

Nikulina, V., Lindal, J.L., Baumann, H., Simon, D. and Ny, H. (2019) 'Lost in translation: a framework for analysing complexity of co-production settings in relation to epistemic communities, linguistic diversities and culture', *Futures*, 113: 102442. doi: 10.1016/j.futures.2019.102442

Novy, A., Habersack, S. and Schaller, B. (2014) 'Innovative forms of knowledge production: transdisciplinarity and knowledge alliance', in F. Moulaert, D. MacCallum, A. Mehmood and A. Hamdouch (eds) *The International Handbook on Social Innovation*, Cheltenham and North Hampton, MA: Edward Elgar, p. 433.

Robinson, J. (2011) 'Cities in a world of cities: the comparative gesture', *International Journal of Urban and Regional Research*, 35(1): 1–23. doi:10.1111/j.1468-2427.2010.00982.x

Robinson, J. (2016) 'Comparative urbanism: new geographies and cultures of theorizing the urban', *International Journal of Urban and Regional Research*, 40(1): 187–99. doi:10.1111/1468–2427.12273

Stavrides, S. (2016) *Common Space: City as Commons*, London: Zed Books.

Wiek, A., Talwar S., O'Shea M.' and Robinson J. (2014) 'Toward a methodological scheme for capturing societal effects of participatory sustainability research', *Research Evaluation*, 23(2): 117–32.

SIX

Internationally initiated projects with local co-production: Urban Sustainable Development Goal project

Sandra C. Valencia, David Simon, Sylvia Croese, Kristina Diprose,

Joakim Nordqvist, Michael Oloko, Tarun Sharma and Ileana Versace

Introduction

Agenda 2030 and its Sustainable Development Goals (SDGs), with the dedicated urban goal SDG 11 and New Urban Agenda (NUA), represent a landmark acknowledgement by the international community of the critical role of cities and other sub-national entities in achieving sustainability. Both the SDGs and NUA will require the engagement of local governments and citizens to be successful. Mistra Urban Futures has been engaged in these processes since 2014 and in 2015 undertook a highly innovative three-month pilot project to test the then draft targets and indicators of what became SDG 11 on sustainable cities and communities. This pilot proved instrumental in deepening several LIPs' partnerships with their respective local authorities, in generating awareness in the city administrations of what would be required in terms of implementation of SDG 11 for the period 2016–30, and also fed directly into modifications to the final versions of several targets and indicators (Simon et al, 2016; Arfvidsson et al, 2017; Patel et al, 2017; Hansson et al, 2019).

The comparative project discussed here commenced in mid-2017 and was a longer sequel to the pilot, designed to follow and support the understanding, engagement and implementation of these two global agendas at the city level. It included seven cities of small to medium size, including all of Mistra Urban Futures' LIPs (Cape Town, Gothenburg, Kisumu, Malmö and Sheffield), plus Shimla in India and Buenos Aires in Argentina through new partnerships with the social enterprise Nagrika and the New School's Observatory on Latin America, respectively. The first three also participated in the pilot project, already well aware of the importance of the agendas to their evolving responsibilities, and the new partnerships in Buenos Aires and Shimla enabled the project to leverage additional value and comparative insights from an even more diverse set of cities on four continents. These cities represent a good microcosm of the many cities worldwide that generally receive far less attention than the small group of 'world cities' and megacities.

The project was conceptualised and designed centrally, adapting the 2015 pilot and reflecting the universal nature of Agenda 2030 and the NUA. The conceptualisation included a guiding framework and set of research questions reflecting the universal nature of Agenda 2030 and the NUA, the indivisibility of the SDGs and a transdisciplinary co-production approach. The project leaders also provided a suggested timeline and deliverables for the rest of the team. In each city, local researchers were appointed to co-produce research with city officials and other city actors. The local researchers were financed either by Mistra Urban Futures or their local platforms, while the work of the city officials was part of their in-kind counterpart to the local platforms work. The local co-production aspect involves adapting the centrally designed project to the local context and agreeing on locally adapted implementation plans (Valencia et al, 2019).

Individual city analyses and comparative outputs were prepared for each city, involving team members from all cities. Two workshops with representatives from all cities were organised to facilitate cross-city learning. The first cross-city workshop took place in Cape Town in November 2018, in which city officials and researchers from all case study cities participated. The second and final cross-city workshop took place in October 2019 in Sheffield. A virtual city–city peer review process was agreed during the Cape Town meeting. The process started in December 2018 with each city submitting a question, concern or proposal concerning a current aspect of the city's involvement in Agenda 2030. Two peer-review cities were assigned to prepare individual responses based on their own experience of working with Agenda 2030 and other relevant sustainability initiatives.

The strategy for and experiences of building an internationally initiated project with local co-production

Transdisciplinary co-production of the project has taken shape uniquely in each city. In Gothenburg, the researcher has been integrated into a group of public officials at the City Executive Office (*Stadsledningskontoret*) assessing how the SDGs relate to the city's ongoing activities and on preparing an Agenda 2030 communications strategy for city politicians and staff. The group and other city departments adapted the project's guiding framework to map how relevant the SDGs are to the city's budget and main strategies, and how the city's 2018 budget goals and strategies can contribute to the SDGs. The Executive Office mapping exercise resulted in a report that was presented and approved by the elected Executive Board in 2018.

In Cape Town, an agreement was signed between the City and the University of Cape Town to embed a researcher into the city's Organisational Policy and Planning Department to engage and work directly with city officials on adapting these agendas. In Shimla, a knowledge partnership was established between the social enterprise, Nagrika, and the Municipal Corporation of Shimla. The Municipal Corporation agreed to be part of the project as long as it could be connected to and complement its current programmes and schemes, particularly the Smart City and Disaster Risk Reduction and Resilience programmes. This helped create greater buy-in and acceptance of the project as well as illuminating the relevance of the Municipal Corporation's own project with regard to international issues of sustainable urban development.

In Buenos Aires, the first step was to build a transdisciplinary team with three main actors: academia (the Observatory on Latin America, a New School initiative hosted by the University of Buenos Aires), civil society (the non-governmental organisation [NGO] Centre for Legal and Social Studies [CELS]) and public sector (the General Directorate of Strategic Management and Institutional Quality, SGEyCI, which is the office in charge of the SDGs within the City of Buenos Aires). The work of this transdisciplinary group started with agreeing the timeline, as well as on a common research focus, given the diverse objectives of each institution. As part of the workplan, tasks are divided between the researchers, NGO partners and city officials, and later reviewed in monthly meetings.

In Kisumu, a working team involving researchers and city and county officials was formed. The project gained the attention of Kenya's national SDG implementation team and, following a meeting between a national delegation and Mistra Urban Futures' director during the 2018 United Nations (UN) High-Level Political Forum in New York as well as a meeting between the SDG national team and the local researcher, interest was confirmed from national-level officials to become linked to the project. Accordingly, Kisumu then became a Kenyan pilot city for local-level implementation of the SDGs. Subsequently, meetings have taken place between the SDG national team, county and city officials and project researche to discuss possibilities and challenges of SDGs' localisation processes and more broadly urban sustainability issues linked to SDG 11 and other relevant targets. The discussions focused on data availability and methodologies for collecting and analysing local indicators. Meetings between representatives at the national level (Kenya National Bureau of Statistics and the Ministry of Planning and Devolution) and the county and city levels were planned twice annually for the duration of the project. Including this project, three-pronged efforts to localise and respond to SDG implementation processes were identified, at the county and city levels, at the national level through the Ministry of Planning and Devolution, and at the county level through the Council of Governors.

A crucial ingredient in all cities was to find a champion or group of key actors open to the potential benefit of engaging with these agendas (Leck and Roberts, 2015). Nevertheless, determining how to anchor the project so that it survives political cycles and associated potential shifts in priorities and power relations proved challenging. In Kisumu and Shimla, the start of the project was delayed due to elections and changing key staff. Similarly, in Cape Town, organisational restructuring within the City delayed the project's launch. Once the project was up and running and interest established with the main city partners, the project started moving more speedily. With or without formal agreements, key personnel changes create the need for familiarisation anew and accommodation to possible changing circumstances within one or more institutions. In Malmö, contractual issues delayed the ability of the local researcher to commence work. Co-production of the project was agreed in 2018 between the local researcher and the city's Sustainability Office, which is in charge of Agenda 2030, but a reorganisational initiative then commenced during 2019. Collectively, these processes affected the co-production arrangements by delaying and then limiting the Sustainability Office's ability to process and follow up on project-related inputs. In Sheffield, where the municipality had not yet started to engage actively with these agendas, establishing a co-production team proved more challenging. Thus, the first step consisted of raising awareness about what these agendas can contribute to city planning, in an effort to galvanise willingness to participate in the project.

A general observation is that even where good working relations exist between researchers and city officials, during busy administrative times, such as the run-up to the end of the financial year, elections, and budget or city development plan preparations, city officials are less likely to engage in the project and project deadlines may be delayed. From the perspective of the researchers (who are the authors of this chapter), it was important to adapt to these local dynamics but also maintain the contact, even during these times, and produce relevant documentation so that the municipality concerned continued to see the project as adding value rather than being a burden.

Benefits and challenges of working with a centrally designed project that is then locally co-produced

Designing the project centrally from the research institute has implications for the rest of the project and the local co-production processes. Given that this project was not requested by city officials, it cannot be said that it was co-designed. It was up to each local researcher or research team to find a suitable counterpart at the city administration and establish a working relationship and work plan that is as co-productive as possible. This also means that in cases where no prior working relations with relevant city officials existed, it was necessary to establish these from scratch, which took time. Setting this up was both facilitated and constrained by the centrally designed nature of the project. Given that the global agendas (Agenda 2030 and NUA) are comprehensive and multi-sectoral, they require a city partner with a sufficiently overarching view and access to the local authority. It is therefore not surprising that most teams have involved city officials at strategic and leading offices such as the planning office, city executive office, or even the head of the municipality itself in the smaller municipalities such as Shimla, where the main counterpart is the commissioner. In the case of Buenos Aires, the local team also involved a specialist human rights NGO. Building trust and a good work plan that suited the needs and interests of the city administration, the NGO and the university took time. The flexibility of the central project, both in terms of initial timeframes (while teams were forming) and content, allowed the local team to achieve good working relations with an agreed working agenda relevant to local needs and to the comparative project.

Using Agenda 2030, in particular, with its universal language and applicability, has helped to interest some municipalities in joining the project, particularly those that had already started working on Agenda 2030 or thought the project could help them getting started with the localisation process. Many cities were not yet working with the SDGs and NUA when the project started. In some, the project provided the impetus for cities to start exploring these agendas and how to implement them locally. In other cities, it made setting up the collaboration arrangements more difficult as officials were busy with other, more pressing issues. In Sheffield, for example, with the SDGs still relatively low-profile at the national level, the focus was on establishing a partnership that could support the local authority's awareness of the SDGs and explore opportunities for engagement. Even in cities where the SDGs have been set as priority by politicians or city officials, such as in Malmö, those charged with working with the SDGs had to carve out their role with limited resources in sceptical or rigid city government environments. These struggles meant that the SDG teams had constantly to be attentive, sensitive and reactive to oppositional responses within the municipal organisation itself and had to focus their engagement to pre-prioritised processes, inadvertently causing inertia when it came to adaptability and quick-footedness in response to secondary or peripheral processes, such as this transdisciplinary research project.

International agendas like the SDGs and NUA are not automatically integrated into national and local policy everywhere. Our research suggests a disconnect between these tiers of government in the UK context, for example. Indeed, the UK experience suggests that where there has been local government engagement with the SDGs (for example in Bristol, Canterbury and Liverpool), this process has been stakeholder-led rather than top-down. Further, despite the project being conceived to cover the local adaptation of the whole Agenda 2030 and the NUA, in Buenos Aires it was necessary to adjust the scope of the research considering the limitations of the main city counterpart. Following the City office's priorities, the team agreed to examine housing issues in depth, a topic that crosses several SDGs as it includes issues of equality, water, electricity and transport, for instance. This led the team to enhance collaboration with the housing institute and the project has facilitated cross-institutional collaboration, an issue with which most cities struggle. These examples highlight the necessity of a local co-production approach adapted to each city's needs and national context.

A key ingredient of the project's comparative element was the team's monthly conference calls, which enabled the local researchers and team leaders to share experiences on the cities' activities and also on methodological challenges and opportunities inherent in carrying out co-production with actors with different levels of awareness and engagement in the global agendas. However, this also meant that the international component of the project was carried out mostly by the researchers, apart from the face-to-face, cross-city sharing events and the city-to-city, peer-review process mentioned earlier. Given that the project embraced seven cities, involving the city staff in frequent virtual meetings would have been very difficult and hard to facilitate. A lesson learned is that if the intention is to have an international comparative project with both researchers and city staff involved throughout the whole process, a smaller number of cities is required. In a project with two to three cities, having regular virtual exchanges between the researcher–city staff teams of each city might be feasible, and a more horizontal and even distribution of responsibilities could be implemented.

At the same time, the international comparative aspect, with cities on four continents all working on global sustainability agendas, was seen by local authorities as an important incentive to being part of the project. Several teams of city officials and researchers highlighted that this made them feel part of a larger and strategic endeavour towards sustainable urban development, where they can contribute to global processes through initiatives in their local work. The variety of cities representing different contexts and starting points for global policy can represent a challenge for cross-city learning. Yet, project city teams underscored the benefits of learning from diverse contexts in various countries, cities, governance arrangements, institutional forms, and policy regimes. Learning across cities was facilitated by the centrally designed project, which provided a window to other approaches through a common framework (the project itself, but also Agenda 2030 and the NUA) for comparison and learning, as well as giving additional legitimacy, credibility and strength to the local work and Agenda 2030 itself. In Cape Town, for example, the engagement of the embedded researcher with actors external to the city on SDGs and NUA implementation was ongoing and greatly appreciated as a source of information and engagement. The sharing of lessons across cities facilitated by the project also offered an opportunity for cities to reflect on their own enterprises and strategies. Sharing of lessons took place not only through the face-to-face meetings in Cape Town and Sheffield and the peer-to-peer review but also through the information shared in the monthly research team virtual meetings, which was then passed on from local researchers to their respective city officials. In short, the project created valuable room for learning and self-reflection, for which there was otherwise very little time in city administrations. It also provided opportunities to position local sustainability work in a global context and strengthen international relationships with other cities.

Even so, it was challenging for some municipalities to understand the larger scenario in which the project activities and outcomes were situated. In other words, the project has had far-reaching and long-term outcomes, while local bodies mainly attend to various immediate local challenges. This occurred particularly in cities with limited devolution responsibilities, such as Shimla, where strategic decisions, such as short- to medium-term development plans, are often the responsibility of higher levels of government, in this case the state. In addition, one challenge of working with internationally agreed agendas and a centrally designed project was making the activities context-specific. The SDGs and NUA reflect the collective priorities of countries and urban areas as a whole, while challenges faced by individual cities are often context-specific, which may or may not tie in with the global priorities.

The fact that the project was centrally designed and administered, outside of the municipal organisation itself, was for several cities, such as Malmö and Sheffield, a prerequisite for participation. In several of the cities, there would have been no resources available for assuming a leading role in such an endeavour. In Cape Town, for example, having an embedded researcher who is paid by Mistra Urban Futures was seen as providing an additional resource for the city to work on Agenda 2030. The international comparison component of the project also mobilised knowledge and resources that would not have been achievable if the project had been a single-city, locally designed project. In Sheffield, for example, the team was able to contrast research findings about low local awareness of the SDGs with examples of how SDG awareness, engagement and localisation have been supported and enabled by national governments in partner cities/countries. Asking the same questions in each country and city enabled the team to realise just how poor the UK government's response to the SDGs has been, and to use cross-national evidence to highlight this through the UK Voluntary National Report process. In Gothenburg, where there has been a limited political mandate regarding Agenda 2030 and where the 2018 elections significantly changed the political landscape and control of the elected city council, precipitating a period of uncertainty for the Agenda 2030 group at the city administration, the project helped provide stability and continuing legitimacy to its work. In Kisumu, in the context of clear national commitments to the SDGs, the project facilitated initiating collaboration and information sharing at the national, county and city levels and with other key stakeholders. As previously mentioned, as a result of the project, the Kenyan national office in charge of SDG implementation chose Kisumu to help it understand how the SDGs are being localised to the city level as a model for other urban areas to emulate.

The centrally designed project also allowed the cities some exposure to perspectives that might not have surfaced had the project been designed by the municipality itself. One vital example was the project's focus on indicators as a core element of analysis. Several of the cities, for example Gothenburg, Malmö and Sheffield, had not initially identified indicators as a focus of their work. The flexibility of the project permitted cities to start the research–practitioner joint work in the areas of common interest. In the cases where the local authority's interest did not match with the project's originally proposed outcomes, it was the researchers' role to complement the joint work to achieve those outcomes. However, in some cases, where data were not available for key indicators such as those under the urban SDG, this was not possible. Even where data were available, but a city had little interest in using the SDGs indicators, local teams recognised that the part of the project focused on indicators ran the risk of becoming an exercise in measuring for measuring's sake rather than exploring more broadly the benefits and drawbacks of the SDGs as a framework for local sustainability planning. Attempting to accommodate these challenges, the project team tried to take a less rigid approach and allow city teams to adapt certain design choices along the way, accepting that the outcomes of the project would vary by city.

Even for cities where the interests of researchers and city officials coincided, institutional capacity could pose challenges in producing the expected outputs for the project, and even beyond the project, having the necessary capacity to meet the localised goals of these global agendas and to monitor progress towards those goals. In Kisumu, for example, data collection for monitoring and evaluation was considered a priority from the inception of the project and the UN-recommended indicators as a good starting point for identifying key data to monitor the three dimensions of sustainability. However, the local team found significant data gaps and a time-lag in updating some of the indicators. It also found a lack of statistical capacity at the city and county levels to compute some of the indicators. An additional challenge relating to indicators, and that applies to all countries, is that not all UN-recommended indicators yet have a defined methodology and thus countries have had to develop their own interpretations of indicators and methodologies while waiting for the globally suggested methods.

Another additional challenge arising from the central project design was that some research questions made assumptions about the existing level of engagement with the SDGs and NUA that did not necessarily reflect reality or local priorities. The NUA exemplified this in almost all cities. The project was designed soon after the NUA's adoption in Quito in October 2016. There was an expectation by the UN that this agenda would resonate in cities and be implemented in parallel to Agenda 2030. However, none of our case study cities had engaged with the NUA by the end of 2019, making the framing of the project about both global agendas and the research questions related to the NUA almost redundant, except that this represents a significant finding in its own right.

A minor potential exception is Buenos Aires, which subscribes to the NUA in a declarative way. Yet, the city administration does not use it as a reference either to review its governmental goals or to assess its results. Since this agenda does not provide interpretative or implementational instruments, it becomes, through the vision of the city team in charge of international commitments, a declaration of interest more than a tool for public management. Indeed, UN-Habitat issued national government reporting guidelines on implementation of the NUA only in June 2019 (UN-Habitat, 2019).

Benefits and challenges of the local co-production process

The researcher–city official knowledge co-production partnerships that were established in each of the project cities had many benefits and distinct results, but they were not devoid of challenges. First, for many city official partners, the concept of knowledge co-production was new, and the project was their first experience of engaging in such an endeavour, as in the case of Shimla. In cities such as Cape Town, where there was already an established knowledge transfer programme between the City and University of Cape Town's African Centre for Cities (see Chapter Four), establishing the co-production partnership was easier and the project contributed to building additional trust and working partnerships that were quickly seen as mutually beneficial. In Kisumu and Gothenburg, cities that also had established collaborations between Mistra Urban Futures' researchers and city administrations, one challenge was the limited local political momentum and budget allocation. Similarly, in a city like Sheffield, where there has been low awareness of the SDGs and no staff or budget allocated to working on Agenda 2030, much of the co-production process was taken up with simply getting a pilot project off the ground.

In several cities, the research team gained access to internal city meetings to discuss the SDGs. This occurred in Gothenburg, where the researcher joined the monthly SDG team meetings at the City Executive Office. This type of access to internal meetings helped maintain frequent contact between the researcher and city officials, as well as access to information and discussions that provided extra insights into why certain things move more quickly than others. It also helped researchers gain a better understanding of how the city administration operates, which includes the opportunities and challenges faced by city officials to act on particular subjects, and their relationships with politicians. The extent to which researchers were able to contribute to internal processes (such as writing or reviewing relevant reports) varied significantly by city, reflecting the different traditions of collaboration between local government and academia and the importance of making international co-production projects flexible in order to adapt the process to the different contexts.

Knowledge co-production and, more generally, under-taking collaborations between different institutions can be challenging. On the one hand, the different institutional arrangements between the partners, reflected in the way the city administrations operate vis-à-vis research institutes and NGOs, can slow the pace of work and require recurrent discussions about the expectations of the collaboration, and the different roles and timeframes. On the other hand, the diverse institutional settings and capacities of the partners involved can also be complementary, which gives the opportunity, particu-larly for the researchers, to find issues or tasks related to the project that are also seen as beneficial for the local government.

Given the novelty of Agenda 2030 for several of the munici-palities at the inception of the project, the local co-production process also included building awareness and capacity within local government, not only of the Agenda itself but also in some cities of goal-based planning. In cities with limited engagement with Agenda 2030, the co-production process gave local authorities additional capacity to think through and start working on the Agenda, while sharing experiences with other cities. Even cities with the reputation of being forerunners in the pursuit of urban sustainability and Agenda 2030, such as Malmö, gained the twin benefits of being considered a contributor to global efforts for localisation of the SDGs, while also becoming both a source and a recipient of knowledge through the local and international co-production processes. This can provide substantial value to the work of the city and the engagement of officials in the knowledge co-production. The raised awareness and additional capacity resulting from the co-production process helped highlight to city officials the importance of universities and other research-focused organisations as anchor institutions for local sustainability planning. This therefore represents a particular variant of the value of city–university partnerships, a subject of considerable current interest (Trencher et al, 2014b, 2014a; Allen et al, 2017; Withycombe Keeler et al, 2018, 2019). Yet, in some cities such as in Malmö and Sheffield, the project period was too short for co-production to emerge not only as an opportunity but also as a practice within the project.

One challenge in most cities was data collection. In the larger cities, such as Buenos Aires, the city administration has several offices involved in the evaluation and monitoring of the SDGs. The positive side is that the city has the capacity to generate its own information, and it has a centralised office, SGEyCI, in charge of the SDG localisation. These characteristics allowed the research team access to official information and to the main department related to the implementation of the Agenda 2030. However, it was challenging to access some specific data produced by other departments. In smaller cities, the challenge was the limited availability of disaggregated city-level data that are reliable and collected regularly.

Another aspect on which all researchers reflected was their positionality, particularly in the cities with limited engagement with these agendas. The co-production process included having to raise awareness of the SDGs and how they might be useful in persuading local partners to undertake the project with the researchers; there is a risk that researchers end up coming across like advocates or SDG consultants rather than critical scientists. In Sheffield, for example, the membership of the research team in the UK Stakeholders for Sustainable Development and the co-organisation of a workshop on localising the SDGs exemplified its ambiguous 'research-as-advocacy' role. It was important for all the research teams to make clear to their city partners that they were not there to 'sell' the SDGs, and they were free to be critical or sceptical of the framework as well as to explore jointly its possible benefits. Similarly, a challenge was how to critically (co-)write about the city and the way it operates without jeopardising established relationships.

Engagement and contribution to Realising Just Cities and Rethinking Sustainable Cities

As Perry and Atherton (2017) note, it is important to ensure that transdisciplinary co-production processes contribute towards the realisation of more socially inclusive, economically viable and ecologically sound cities. We could argue that this project contributed by enabling cities to reflect on how the planning processes contribute to the latter objectives and to set up monitoring frameworks to measure progress towards those objectives. The extent to which planning processes actually change thanks to the co-production process in the context of Agenda 2030 developed in this project remains to be seen. One aspect where we can point to some limitations is that of social inclusiveness, not necessarily in terms of the social policies of each study city, but rather on the inclusiveness of different actors in the process of localising global agendas to the city level. While the project contributed in several cities to promoting cross-sectoral dialogues to discuss Agenda 2030, those dialogues were mostly limited to city departments, with little engagement of other actors outside the city administration, such as civil society and the private sector. One clear exception was Buenos Aires, where several actors were engaged both in awareness raising and in writing a report on how different actors understand and can use Agenda 2030. That broad engagement process had started even prior to this project, which, nevertheless, contributed to intersectoral discussions, particularly on housing-related issues.

Both the NUA and Agenda 2030 call for participatory processes. In the case of the SDGs, SDG 11.3 explicitly calls for participatory planning. The NUA has not yet found echo in our case study cities and, as previously mentioned, in most cities SDG localisation has been focused on the city administration, but it is too early to tell whether SDGs will drive more participatory and inclusive processes. Our project focused by design on how the city administrations were localising the SDGs and the NUA, so, in most cases, the project has not directly contributed to more participatory or inclusive processes.

To contribute to inclusive planning processes, these types of projects might need to include a civil society and/or private sector co-production partner. This would increase some of the local challenges mentioned here, make the process slower and the international comparison and exchange more challenging. At the same time, including additional co-production partners could potentially contribute more directly to inclusiveness, which is one aspect of just cities as embodied in Mistra Urban Futures' Realising Just Cities framework (Chapters Two and Eight). Even so, increasing the number of co-production partners could empower those partners and have positive effects on the partners and those actors they influence or with whom they work with; it does not guarantee that the process would lead to city-wide social inclusion.

The experience of this project, therefore, shows that co-production processes around broad agendas that aim for sustainability, inclusion and justice can contribute to the ability of city officials to reflect on and question the status quo, assess their municipality's baseline, identify gaps and set up goals. These are arguably the first steps for rethinking sustainable cities (Simon, 2016). One challenge is how to extend the co-production from the research team and a limited set of city officials to changing the way that a municipality operates in general. To that extent, it is important not to make assumptions about what form the cities' future engagement with the SDGs or the NUA might take. There is a risk that it may lack momentum and local political support, not because anyone disagrees with these global agendas, but because there are other local priorities and established local equivalents in situations of constrained resources. A forward plan for engagement with both agendas would have to be locally owned and resourced to be sustainable beyond the life of our project, mindful of the ongoing capacity constraints and budget cuts that local authorities face.

References

Allen, J.H., Beaudoin, F. and Gilden, B. (2017) 'Building powerful partnerships: lessons from Portland's Climate Action Collaborative', *Sustainability: The Journal of Record*, 10(5): 276–81. doi: 10.1089/sus.2017.0010

Arfvidsson, H., Simon, D., Oloko, M. and Moodley, N. (2017) 'Engaging with and measuring informality in the proposed Urban Sustainable Development Goal', *African Geographical Review*, 36(1): 100–14. doi: 10.1080/19376812.2015.1130636

Hansson, S., Arfvidsson, H. and Simon, D. (2019) 'Governance for sustainable urban development: the double function of SDG indicators', *Area Development and Policy*, 4(20): 1–19. doi: 10.1080/23792949.2019.1585192

Leck, H. and Roberts, D. (2015) 'What lies beneath: understanding the invisible aspects of municipal climate change governance', *Current Opinion in Environmental Sustainability*, 13: 61–7. doi:10.1016/j.cosust.2015.02.004

Patel, Z., Greyling, S., Simon, D., Arfvidsson, H., Moodley, N., Primo, N. and Wright, C. (2017) 'Local responses to global sustainability agendas: learning from experimenting with the urban sustainable development goal in Cape Town', *Sustainability Science*, 12(5): 785–97. doi:10.1007/s11625-017-0500-y

Perry, B. and Atherton, M. (2017) 'Beyond critique: the value of co-production in realising just cities?', *Local Environment*, 22(July): 36–51. doi:10.1080/13549839.2017.1297389

Simon, D., Arfvidsson, H., Anand, G., Bazaz, A., Fenna, G., Foster, K., Jain, G., Hansson, S., Evans, L.M., Moodley, N., Nyambuga, C., Oloko, M., Ombara, D.C., Patel, Z. et al (2016) 'Developing and testing the Urban Sustainable Development Goals targets and indicators – a five-city study', *Environment and Urbanization*, 28(1): 49–63. doi:10.1177/0956247815619865

Simon, D. (ed) (2016) *Rethinking Sustainable Cities: Accessible, Green and Fair*, Bristol: Policy Press. Available from: https://oapen.org/se arch?identifier=613676;keyword=Rethinking%20Sustainable%20 Cities

Trencher, G., Bai, X., Evans, J., McCormick, K. and Yarime, M. (2014a) 'University partnerships for co-designing and co-producing urban sustainability', *Global Environmental Change*, 28(1): 153–65. doi: 10.1016/j.gloenvcha.2014.06.009

Trencher, G., Yarime, M., McCormick, K.B., Doll, C.N.H. and Kraines, S.B. (2014b) 'Beyond the third mission: exploring the emerging university function of co-creation for sustainability', *Science and Public Policy*, 41(2): 151–79. doi: 10.1093/scipol/sct044

UN-Habitat (United Nations Human Settlements Programme) (2019) *Guidelines for Reporting on the Implementation of the New Urban Agenda*, Nairobi: UN-Habitat.

Valencia, S., Simon, D., Croese, S., Nordqvist, J., Oloko, M., Sharma, T., Taylor Buck, N. and Versace, I. (2019) 'Adapting the Sustainable Development Goals and the New Urban Agenda to the city level: initial reflections from a comparative research project', *International Journal of Urban Sustainable Development*, 11(1): 4–23. doi: 10.1080/19463138.2019.1573172

Withycombe Keeler, L., Beaudoin, F., Lerner, A., John, B., Beecroft, R., Tamm, K., Wiek, A. and Lang, D. (2018) 'Transferring sustainability solutions across contexts through city–university partnerships', *Sustainability*, 10(9): 2966. doi: 10.3390/su10092966

Withycombe Keeler, L., Beaudoin, F., Wiek, A., John, B., Lerner, A.M., Beecroft, R., Tamm, K., Seebacher, A., Lang, D.J., Kay, B. and Forrest, N. (2019) 'Building actor-centric transformative capacity through city–university partnerships', *Ambio*, 48(5): 529–38. doi: 10.1007/s13280-018-1117-9

SEVEN

Participatory cities from the 'outside in': the value of comparative learning

Beth Perry and Bert Russell

Introduction

Recent academic work on comparison has decentred strict comparative studies, where the aim is to produce generalisable knowledge on the basis of seeking standardised units of analysis and careful control of variables. While such work continues to be important and has its place in generating better evidence about 'what works' beyond single case studies, attention has turned to other forms of comparison, as explored in Chapter Two. Increasingly, the emphasis has been on the purpose of comparison beyond generalisation, with a specific focus on the value of learning. One conceptualisation describes the 'import mirror' view (May and Perry, 2010: 249) which suggests that 'the project of comparative analysis is worthwhile because in producing findings on the practices of other countries, we are better able to see the basis of our own practices'. Through this lens, we can reflect on our social systems and cultural ways of behaving, which take different social contexts and cultural practices into account. These ideas also underpin

Colin McFarlane's work, which emphasises the importance of comparison and learning for political strategies and progressive urbanism (McFarlane, 2011).

Reframing what we mean by comparison, and how it is undertaken, is particularly important given the increasing focus on engaging stakeholders meaningfully in the design, conduct and analysis of research in the context of the 'co-productive turn'. Recent work emphasises how co-produced methodologies need to be sufficiently open in their design (Perry et al, 2019) to be 'palpably affected' (Fung and Wright, 2001) by participants. As elaborated in relation to diverse research designs in earlier chapters, even where there may be an initial standardisation of approach, co-production introduces potential differentiation in design and method according to the needs of local stakeholders.

Questions must also be raised about who is supported to undertake comparison in co-production projects. International travel has traditionally been accepted as part of the legitimate work of academia, while local government officials and civil society members do not have access to the same resources or permissions to travel and have been under greater pressure to defend such decisions. Who owns and benefits from comparison and how this enables action on the ground are key challenges for those involved in co-produced research.

This chapter documents an alternative approach to co-producing comparison to draw out the value of collaborative comparative learning. The chapter contributes an otherwise overlooked perspective to the themes in the book by setting out how to support urban policy makers in comparative learning that can help them better understand and reflect on their own policy and practice. It draws on a knowledge exchange activity organised as part of the Mistra Urban Futures work stream on Participatory Cities to provide a lens on the wider issues. The activity involved two local government officials, two academics and two citizens of Greater Manchester (GM), UK, forming a delegation to the November 2018 International

Observatory on Participatory Democracy (IOPD) conference held in Barcelona. The delegation attended sessions, organised a joint workshop and identified key learning points from the conference to share in Greater Manchester. Data are drawn from a transcript of a reflective discussion among the six delegation members to highlight stakeholder views on the types and value of comparative learning. Four themes are identified: learning about participatory democracy; reflecting on policy and practice; grounding progress in international perspective; and opening the horizons of possibility.

The chapter concludes that the purpose of comparison in co-production is not only about the production of generalisable knowledge. In keeping with the ethos of 'doing with' and 'not to', involving urban officials and stakeholders in the generation of comparative insights, can enable learning from the outside in. By 'outside in', we mean using insights from other urban settings to better understand conditions, constraints, limits and possibilities in one's own context. Enabling local stakeholders to participate directly in comparative learning activities accelerates the transfer of relevant lessons that may support the realisation of more just cities.

While co-production often aspires to engage stakeholders throughout the whole knowledge process, the chapter argues that comparative learning should be prioritised over more specialised aspects of the research process, such as data analysis or academic writing, especially when there are limits on stakeholders' ability to commit time and resources to research. The chapter evidences the value of comparative learning from the 'outside in' and the need to find novel mechanisms to open up policy imaginations. Transdisciplinary co-production has a role to play in ensuring that comparison can benefit urban officials in their decision making in the context of increasingly limited resources and constraints. In line with the ethos of this book, the chapter has been written to appeal to a wide audience, drawing on academic ideas to stimulate wider reflection on the process and value of comparative policy learning.

Towards 'meaningful participation'

In an epoch where inequality is becoming increasingly severe on a global scale (Piketty, 2013), and in which far-right nationalisms and populism are becoming dominant, the search for solutions that are just – in both process and outcomes – is as urgent as ever. The search for the just city (Fainstein, 2013) means taking seriously urban structural and institutional conditions and governance arrangements. Attention must be paid to the organisation of cities, foregrounding questions around the design and ownership of municipal institutions. Different forms of citizen participation, ranging from citizen involvement in urban planning processes through to municipal energy strategies, neighbourhood budgets or citizen juries, have been supported by local governments. However, in the context of multiple challenges to the idea of the 'nation state' and variable decentralisation and devolution efforts, greater citizen engagement has adopted an almost panacea-like character, capable 'not only … of addressing issues of poverty and social justice; it is also a means of tackling the growing democratic deficit that is now widely discussed in both "mature" and "emerging" democracies' (Gaventa, 2004: 26).

The New Urban Agenda and the Sustainable Development Goals

As detailed in Chapter Six, acknowledgement of the importance of participation and the role of local governments has been embedded in both the United Nations' New Urban Agenda (NUA) and the Sustainable Development Goals (SDGs). Running through the NUA is a clear commitment that its vision requires the 'empowering [of] all individuals and communities while enabling their full and meaningful participation' (UN-Habitat, 2016, para 26). This is made most explicit in one of the 'transformative commitments for sustainable urban development', which asserts the primacy of:

... promoting institutional, political, legal and financial mechanisms in cities and human settlements to broaden inclusive platforms, in line with national policies, that allow *meaningful* participation in decision-making, planning and follow-up processes for all, as well as enhanced civil engagement and co-provision and co-production. (UN-Habitat, 2016: 14, emphasis added)

Similarly, SDG 16 focuses on 'ensuring responsive, inclusive, participatory and representative decision-making at all levels'. However, while the NUA and SDGs should be considered as 'an achievement in terms of bringing global attention to the critical importance of cities for humanity and its future', there appears to be a 'deliberate vagueness in the indicator framework' that suggests the urban SDG – and perhaps the wider SDG framework – is best approached 'as a "proxy" and policy tool, a way to simplify critical issues for the purposes of clarity and activism' (Klopp and Petretta , 2017: 96). Notwithstanding such concerns, a central message from international frameworks is to take the conditions for participation and inclusion of citizens in decision making seriously, as enabling wider sustainable urban transformations.

From co-production to comparison and back again

For these reasons, one of the comparative projects supported by Mistra Urban Futures focused on Participatory Cities. Workshops were held in 2017 in Kisumu, Kenya, that aimed to identify and support common cross-cutting themes around which international comparative work could be developed, with the aspiration of adding value to local projects already under way. The Participatory Cities workshop was attended by over 30 academic and city representatives from Cape Town, Kisumu, Malmö/Skåne, Stockholm, Gothenburg and Sheffield. The workshop was structured around presentations, discussions and workshop exercises to tease out the cultural and epistemic differences in how participation was understood, researched and developed in practice across all six urban contexts.

As noted in other chapters, the initiation of comparative work was influenced by a number of constraining factors, largely relating to the fact that the majority of resources had already been allocated to local co-production projects by each local partnership. Limited additional networking funds were available centrally. Participatory Cities was developed as a series of related work streams, to pull together existing activity on participation in urban governance, decision making and planning from across the different Mistra Urban Futures Local Interaction Platforms (LIPs) – see Chapter One.

The development of comparative work in Phase Two of Mistra Urban Futures was layered on top of existing local co-production work. A critical consideration was therefore what value international perspectives could add to each local interaction platform. Rather than initiate new projects, this meant overlaying local work, co-designed with urban stakeholders, with an international dimension (see Simon et al, 2018). Three different approaches were used: twinning, comparative interviewing and international policy exchanges.

Given that local projects were already underway, the opportunity for comparative work around Participatory Cities also meant thinking through how local partners could be involved and how the opportunity for comparative learning could be aligned with ongoing trajectories. This is now illustrated using the example of Greater Manchester.

Co-producing comparative learning in Greater Manchester

Greater Manchester is a city region with a population of 2.8 million people in northern England, comprised of ten separate local authorities or 'districts'. These districts had collaborated on a voluntary basis since 1986, through a body called the Association of Greater Manchester Authorities.

Following the negotiation of a City Deal in 2012, Greater Manchester became the first English city region outside London to secure greater devolved powers in areas such as transport, planning and housing, on condition that the local authorities agreed to a directly elected metropolitan mayor. The first mayor of Greater Manchester, Andy Burnham, was elected in May 2017 on a manifesto that promised a different relationship between local public authorities and citizens in Greater Manchester. His 'cabinet' comprised himself and the ten local authority leaders, under a new organisation called the Greater Manchester Combined Authority (GMCA).

Such developments have been the subject of many academic studies and are well documented elsewhere (Haughton et al, 2016; Kenealy, 2016; Hodson et al, 2019). Of relevance to this chapter is the coincidence of the initiation of Participatory Cities with this period of huge governance flux, changing national–local relations and questions over how the new mayor would exercise his mandate and engage directly with citizens. In this context, there was an increasing appetite from some city officials to find 'new' ideas and approaches and to open up thinking to alternative approaches to participation.

This context forms the background to the co-production of a knowledge exchange programme between the GMCA and academic researchers involved in the Sheffield–Manchester LIP (SMLIP). In January 2018, discussions began to formulate a coherent 'gateway' for decision makers at the GMCA to collaborate with a wide range of local projects supported by the SMLIP. A process called Developing Co-Productive Capacities was co-designed and co-funded to enable knowledge exchange and to facilitate the engagement of officials in the LIP as a whole. Basket funding for the process was secured from impact funds allocated by participating universities (Sheffield, Manchester and Birmingham) and by aligning existing local spend for knowledge exchange within a range of projects. Match funding in-kind was agreed in the form of officer time and the provision of venues. The negotiation of this year-long process took over three months, with high-level sign-offs required to enable city officials to participate in activities and the identification of key personnel to take part. While delaying the initiation of some parts of the process, this led to strong buy-in and credible commitment, as well as high interest in the results of analysis. Importantly, the negotiation of a *process* for co-producing comparative learning constituted a single mechanism, with institutional endorsement, through which local overlaying of international perspectives could take place.

A central part of Developing Co-productive Capacities was the identification of three learning opportunities for city officials and stakeholders to undertake comparative learning. While comparison is usually undertaken by academic researchers, who then distil and represent relevant lessons back to urban officials, Participatory Cities sought to disrupt this division of labour by enabling stakeholders to engage in direct, unmediated comparative learning. The first learning visit was to the Mistra Urban Futures' annual conference in Cape Town in November 2018, during which Greater Manchester and Gothenburg officials were invited to present their urban contexts and governance arrangements.[1] The second visit shortly thereafter involved a mixed delegation from Greater Manchester to the IOPD meeting in Barcelona. The third was a three-day learning visit to Gothenburg with a wider delegation including citizens, third sector representatives, activists and local officials from Greater Manchester, as well as from the West Midlands Combined Authority.[2] A condition of participation was that participants would write blogs on their reflections and commit to internal workshops to ensure that learning was embedded in wider institutional contexts.[3] To comprehend the value attributed to these exchanges by local stakeholders, the next section focuses specifically on the November 2018 trip to the IOPD to provide a microcosm of the wider issues.[4]

The International Observatory on Participatory Democracy

The IOPD is a network of over 800 cities in 91 countries collaborating to improve local participatory democracy and describes itself as 'a space open to all cities in the world and all associations, organisations and research centres interested in learning about, exchanging impressions and applying experiences of participatory democracy on a local scale with the aim of deepening the roots of democracy in municipal government'.[5] The network was officially founded in 2001 and in 2006 co-ordinated closely with the United Cities and Local Governments global municipal membership organisation, also headquartered in Barcelona, to provide strategic intelligence on participatory democracy.

Annual conferences have been one strand of the IOPD's work to create a space for exchanging practices among members. IOPD conferences require much preparation and many sessions are dedicated to joint decision making and planning between member cities to progress the core work of the organisation. Although there are hundreds of global members, there are very few from the UK– the only local authority listed as a member is Bristol City Council, along with three academic-affiliated organisations and three consultancies/social enterprises.[6] Through the Participatory Cities initiative, the University of Sheffield's Urban Institute had become an associate member, but had not previously attended or been involved in any aspect of the IOPD. Notably, the conference was neither academic in nature nor was held in a space owned by any of the Greater Manchester delegation participating. One delegate reflected that this meant the experience was far more co-operative, flat and equal than it otherwise would have been.

In mid-2018, as part of the Developing Co-productive Capacities process agreed with the GMCA, it was decided to send a delegation to the planned IOPD conference comprising two academics, two GMCA officials and two citizen/civil society co-researchers. The focus was the co-design and delivery of a workshop – 'How to co-produce the city' – which eventually comprised a joint scene-setting presentation and an adapted world café-style exercise. The workshop was recorded on video and a short summary is available online (https://youtu.be/RebvaBaMXMQ). This approach and workshop were unusual in the context of the conference as a whole, where predominately academic *or* practice sessions were delivered, but rarely combined.

The IOPD conference was organised according to three key themes: direct democracy, citizen initiative and ecosystems of inclusive democracy. In total, there were 50 sessions on offer around these key themes. The delegation discussed and agreed collectively which sessions each member would attend, to achieve a good coverage and fit with individuals' areas of interest. Each person agreed to take notes and reflect on relevant lessons and insights for Greater Manchester. On the last evening of the conference, all the participants discussed their reflections and insights in a two-hour group discussion that was audio-recorded and subsequently transcribed. The data from the reflection discussion are presented in the following section. Quotes from delegates are denoted D1, D2, D3 and D4. Given the small number of participants, and based on feedback, job roles are not attributed, in order to preserve anonymity.

Reflections from the conference

The array of case studies, tools and techniques presented at the conference stimulated wide curiosity and interest in what other cities were doing. The volume of activity by local authorities and urban actors in cities around the world served to legitimise an agenda around participatory democracy that has less current coverage in the UK context. Our delegation reflected on the specific challenges facing different urban areas – for instance in cross-border spaces between France and Germany where multiple regional identities are present – and on the different extents to which citizens' initiatives, such as referenda, are binding in different urban contexts.

Beyond specific examples of tools and techniques that could be applied in Greater Manchester, the conference opened up conceptual questioning about participatory democracy and different ways of thinking about participation: "I found that very useful" (D2). While desk-based reviews of the literature had previously been carried out, for instance, outlining the differences between participatory and deliberative democracy, the impact of hearing cities speak directly enabled such ideas to land more powerfully.

Delegates' reflections on the conference echoed wider intellectual concerns regarding the purpose and outcomes of participation:

> 'I would love to see the outcomes of some of these things. Because that's where it never went. So they named a square after something. Or they agreed to have a community garden. Is that where we are here? Or is there something better coming out?' (D1)

Critical questioning followed, supporting a bridging of perspectives between different members of the delegation. For instance, through the experiences of other cities in developing ecosystems of participation, delegates "noticed that feminism and gender identity had been placed at the core of a lot of these conversations about democracy (D3)", something that also reflected one of the political priorities of Barcelona City Council. However, they reflected that questions of race were not similarly central. While struck, on the one hand, by the "radicalness" of what was being presented, this was accompanied by concern at a parallel "lack of radicalness" given the "bigger, more urgent challenges at stake" (D2).

One delegate reflected that the composition of attendees was significant in this respect, noting that there was little consideration of "citizens" within the conference itself. Conference participants presented themselves in their professional roles and city officials "talk about citizens as if citizens are 'over there'". This delegate also noted the importance of leading by example and the need for skills and capacities to make participation real rather than symbolic: "there's something ironic about attending something called the International Observatory on Participatory Democracy and participating in nothing, other than being a passive recipient of information" (D4).

This led to a questioning of whether the agenda around local participatory democracy was "ducking the big questions" (D2). Listening to a presentation on local community participation in Mozambique – a context that was not initially presumed to offer comparative insight to Greater Manchester – this delegate reflected that there was a general lack of prioritisation at the conference. Municipal authorities were foregrounding initiatives that gave citizens control over parks or community squares, through mechanisms such as participatory budgeting, but issues of homelessness or drug addiction were absent from the agenda.

Reflections on what was heard in different sessions led the discussion naturally to the relevance for Greater Manchester. These implications were motivated by initial concerns to replicate or avoid the practices of other cities. For instance, one delegate reflected on the role of intermediary organisations in supporting smaller and under-resourced municipalities, concluding that "one of the things I'll take back is to what extent we can support our Voluntary, Community and Social Enterprise sector to organise and to be able to engage with us, not [on an] equal level, but with some legitimacy" (D1). Delegates found specific interventions relevant and useful – such as the role of digital decision-making tools, participatory indicators or participant-led evaluation as a process for building power.

Understanding the priorities of other municipalities enabled delegates to think back on policy and practice in Greater Manchester. An awareness of the knowledge gaps was shared – while there is "no shortage of ways of doing it", one delegate asked, "Does Greater Manchester understand what the different approaches are? Does GMCA understand it? And are we evaluating what works for our citizens?" (D2). Delegates specifically noted the need to centre the "participation of people who are really struggling and on the breadline" (D2) as well as engage with ideas around participatory budgeting, youth engagement and the SDG agenda. Specific city experiences, such as those of Barcelona,[7] provoked a different policy imagination, but one grounded in an understanding of contextual difference. For one city official, the prospects of radical change are far from Greater Manchester: "Our democratic system is what it is, that's not going to change any time soon. Ours is about broadening what we already have" (D1). This assessment was based on reflecting on the different roles, responsibilities and resources of municipal governments and specifically the limits of the current devolution agreement:

'One of the challenges you have with local government is you are seen as everything to all people at all times, when actually, we have quite defined powers and responsibilities. And even when we want to go beyond and strengthen some of those and work in different ways, there's a limitation of what you can do … we have a role, which is not everything.' (D1)

How to take control and organise "without seeking permission" was the take-away message for another delegate (D3):

'Ada Colau [mayor of Barcelona] was talking about people organising themselves without seeking permission … that being something we should all value and appreciate rather than being scared of it and threatened by it.'

While many urban officials want to identify best practice, the dialogue around replicability was nuanced through the self-identification of constraining and enabling conditions and contexts. Our delegation was struck by the extent of institutional support for participation in other municipalities, where there were full departments for participation or participation officers: "that was something that was seriously committed to, there was resource, there was capacity" (D1). This provoked reflection on whether such an initiative should be owned by city-regional or local authorities and whether, if desirable, it was possible in the context of austerity: "I used to be paid to do it, way back when, when we had a lot more money".

Attendance at the IOPD drew back the veil on the scale and scope of municipalities' active engagement with the theory and practice of participatory democracy in other parts of the world. A central take-home message was that Greater Manchester needs to pay attention to this and consider whether and how to participate in such networks:

> 'We need to connect more and we need to be an importer of ideas. Places are ahead of Greater Manchester on this. We need to take stock of some of what we have heard and also reach into that network.' (D1)

The vibrancy of the network in supporting cross-local learning stood in stark contrast to the current situation in the UK where the urban policy context encourages more competition than collaboration or sharing of practice (May and Perry, 2018).

The experience grounded the need for a less 'boosterist' discourse[8] that seeks to reflect honestly on Greater Manchester's strengths and weaknesses and learn from others. It also enabled delegates to frame what a coherent Greater Manchester contribution could look like. Notably, in the context of multiple discussions about participatory democracy generally, there was very little discussion about co-production in democratic ecosystems of participation: "It's also about putting GM out there. We have dipped our toes in the water talking about co-production today" (D2).

The combination of concrete learning about participatory democracy with reflections on GM's policy and practice in international perspective served both to confirm and challenge existing trajectories. One consequence was to open up discussion about the horizons of possibility beyond the now, to where GM might want to be in the future. "It ranged from things we have done in the past ... things we might do in the future ... and then things which are beyond our current contexts" (D1). The challenges of ceding power and engaging with citizens led to reflection on the need for greater social movement building on GM:

> 'Whether that was Peru, or it was in America, or in unions ... the question for GM is to what extent do we facilitate or put up barriers to that type of social action? Is that in our destiny and where does legislation fit within that as a city region? Generally, we are governed by what's agreed at a national level. So are we a blocker to that sort of movement?' (D2)

One delegate acknowledged that organised social movements can help cities move forward progressively and "that's not always a bad thing". Inspired by examples in Barcelona and Berlin of cities and citizens taking control of their energy or water infrastructure, delegates returned to the issues of risk aversion and embracing social movements. This stimulated wider discussion about the preconditions for wider urban transformations.

> 'That's the question for us: how do we really engage our citizens around the big issues? And are we prepared that people will galvanise and come with alternatives, try and push the system and push ourselves?' (D2)

Honest reflection on institutional cultures within existing organisations followed, noting the need for cultural change and support for city officials and professionals to undertake participation:

> 'The problem is, we always get the answers we are expecting to get when we ask people … and actually maybe we need to start asking different questions. If we want new ideas, how on earth do we go about asking different questions or allowing different spaces or whatever it might be … for those curveballs to start coming through to "wow, there's actually an idea that no one had seen". Where do we get these ideas coming through?' (D1)

Centring the knowledge and skills of citizens in this respect was seen to be key:

> 'We don't go outside of our boundaries in that way, when we think about the skillset of our communities. When it comes to thinking creatively about solutions to tackle some real big issues, what do people bring from communities?' (D1)

Discussion: the value of comparative learning

Through this discussion, we can identify four key themes relating to the value of comparative learning. First, the approach enabled learning about participatory democracy through direct engagement with specific tools, techniques, approaches and methods. Second, delegates reflected on policy and practice in their own context, through honest consideration on the strengths and limits of existing approaches. Rather than looking for 'quick fixes' or models that could be transferred from context to context, comparative learning enabled context-specific lessons to be drawn building on pre-existing understandings of institutional constraints and possibilities. Third, looking from the 'outside in' meant that progress could be then grounded in international experiences and perspectives. This enabled better understanding of where there were learning opportunities and where Greater Manchester had a distinctive offer to make. Fourth, and importantly, the experience started to open up discussion on different horizons of possibility for action and the necessary institutional and cultural changes required to bring them about.

Space was created for urban officials and stakeholders to think outside their usual constraints. One delegate referred to such learning as a 'luxury' not afforded in their everyday professional settings. Attending the conference and being exposed to ideas was valuable, but the post-conference discussion was the key mechanism through which exposure translated to learning. In the reflective dialogue, delegates prompted, questioned and challenged each other, for instance in relation to ideas of what was or wasn't deemed 'possible' in Greater Manchester. Members of the same local governance organisation had the opportunity to engage with each other's ideas and perspectives in ways that were not seen to be feasible at work. Stimulating critical thinking and space for reflection was as valuable as concrete tools and actions.

Collective experience and discussion had other impacts, in strengthening relationships between delegates. Rather than a critical agenda owned solely by academics, a greater shared problem space and critical lens started to develop among delegates. Learning together built trust that affected the quality of the co-productive relationships locally. This was designed from the outset within the wider Developing Co-productive Capacities process. While this chapter builds on a single moment within this process, the themes and values of comparative learning are echoed in the process as a whole. This exchange was only possible as part of a wider negotiated learning partnership that was signed off within GMCA, and due to pre-existing academic–civil society collaborations. Since the IOPD conference, the delegates have continued to work together locally – building a coalition for change to

#CoProduceGM, developing policy commitments towards communities of practice in co-production and co-designing an international policy exchange on co-producing urban policy.

On co-producing comparison

When resources for comparative learning are scarce, where does this leave participatory urban decision making? Urban officials are time-poor and institutional constraints limit the opportunities for learning about what is happening elsewhere, or reflecting on institutional conditions. Similarly, civil society engagement in decision-making processes relies on individuals giving their time voluntarily. Comparison is usually left in the hands of academics who are charged with transferring knowledge to potential users in the form of case studies or examples of best practice. Academics are used to populating international spaces and have had the relative luxury of time and space to think comparatively.

This chapter opens up a debate about what comparison means in co-production and who undertakes it. In this example, comparative learning was co-produced between different individuals from academia, government and civil society organisations through a shared collective experience and reflection. Comparison served to generate thinking from the 'outside in' on the need for, approaches to and possibilities for creating more participatory cities. By undertaking comparison in this way, learning is better embedded in local organisations aiding the exchange of knowledge between academic researchers and urban stakeholders. It simultaneously strengthens trust and relationships as a precondition for better co-productive partnerships locally over time.

On the basis of this experience, we reflect that current knowledge on co-production is not sufficiently sensitive to issues associated with comparison. Structured comparison aimed at generalisation is important to generate better knowledge about 'what works', but is resource-intensive and requires specialised skills (Richardson et al, 2019). Participatory methods do exist to undertake such comparative studies in a more inclusive way in the research process. However, being trained to undertake such tasks is not always desirable or possible for those within an organisation to engage with transdisciplinary knowledge co-production. Comparative learning is not a replacement for systematic analysis, but can support better understanding of different possibilities and prospects for cities beyond the best practice case.

This opens a new avenue of consideration for those concerned with implementing and evaluating the United Nations' urban SDG and New Urban Agenda, and the particular commitment to 'meaningful' participation. Our experience suggests that while traditional technologies of participation such as participatory budgeting (see Chapter Two) or people's assemblies are specific instances of meaningful participation, we must also strive to create boundary spaces that facilitate reflective 'out-of-context experiences'. While the former are often promoted by institutions such as the World Bank (see Goldfrank, 2012), such replicable off-the-shelf techniques provide little substantial challenge to the governing status quo on their own. Comparative learning, when allied with a critical orientation, may provide more important opportunities for subtle moments of rupture to dominant governing logics to be aired, discussed and promoted. If meaningful participation is to be more than a shoring up of business as usual, this suggests that processes of co-produced comparative learning should be taken seriously, if we are to move 'beyond critique' (Perry and Atherton, 2017) and realise the potential of participatory cities.

Acknowledgements

Thanks to the following people for participating in this process: Jacob Botham, David Rogerson, Katie Finney and Alice Toomer Mc-Alpine. The use of the data solely reflects the views and interpretations of the authors.

Notes

[1] www.mistraurbanfutures.org/en/event/RJC2018

[2] https://realisingjustcities-rjc.org/blog/co-production-working-local-democracy and https://realisingjustcities-rjc.org/blog/changing-world-learning-and-reflections-gothenburg-visit

[3] See, for example, https://realisingjustcities-rjc.org/blog/greater-manchester-barcelona-and-back-again-lessons-co-production-and-digital-democracy and https://realisingjustcities-rjc.org/blog/how-co-produce-city-no-easy-steps

[4] At the time of securing the book contract, the Gothenburg learning visit had not taken place.

[5] www.iodp.net/en

[6] Information correct as listed on website www.iodp.net/en September 2019.

[7] The election of Barcelona en Comú in the 2015 municipal elections has led to Barcelona being seen as 'a flagship of [a] new municipalist movement' (Russell, 2019: 992), one in which the relationship between citizens and the state has been a central focus for transformation.

[8] Associated with the emergence of the 'entrepreneurial city' from the mid-1980s onwards (Hall and Hubbard, 1996), city boosterism encapsulates the range of 'place-making' behaviours, such as the rush to host major sporting events (Cochrane et al, 1996), orientated towards the attraction of capital investment.

References

Cochrane, A., Peck, J. and Tickell, A. (1996) 'Manchester plays games: exploring the local politics of globalisation', *Urban Studies*, 33(8): 1319–36.

Fainstein, S. (2013) 'The just city,' *International Journal of Urban Sciences*, 18(1): 1–18. doi: 10.1080/ 12265934.2013.834643

Fung, A. and Wright, E.O. (2001) 'Deepening democracy: innovations in empowered participatory governance', *Politics & Society*, 29(1): 5–41.

Gaventa, J. (2004) 'Strengthening participatory approaches to local governance: learning the lessons from abroad', *National Civic Review*, Winter: 16–27.

Goldfrank, B. (2012) 'The World Bank and the globalization of participatory budgeting', *Journal of Public Deliberation*, 8(2): 1–18.

Hall, T. and Hubbard, P. (1996) 'The entrepreneurial city: new urban politics, new urban geographies?', *Progress in Human Geography*, 20(2): 153–74.

Haughton, G., Deas, I., Hincks, S. and Ward, K. (2016) 'Mythic Manchester: Devo Manc, the Northern Powerhouse and rebalancing the English economy', *Regions, Economy and Society*, 9(2): 355–570.

Hodson, M., McMeekin, A., Froud, J. and Moran, M. (2019) 'State-rescaling and re-designing the material city-region: tensions of disruption and continuity in articulating the future of Greater Manchester', *Urban Studies*, 1–20. doi: 10.1177/0042098018820181

Kenealy, D. (2016) 'A tale of one city: the Devo Manc deal and its implications for English devolution', *Political Quarterly*, 87(4): 572–81.

Klopp, J. and Petretta, D. (2017) 'The urban sustainable development goal: indicators, complexity and the politics of measuring cities', *Cities*, 63(1): 92–7.

May, T. and Perry, B. (2010) 'Comparative research: potentials and problems', in T. May (ed) *Social Research: Issues, Methods and Process*, Maidenhead: Open University Press and McGraw-Hill.

May, T. and Perry, B. (2018) *Cities and the Knowledge Economy: Promise, Politics and Possibilities*, Oxford: Routledge.

McFarlane, C. (2011) *Learning the City: Knowledge and Translocal Assemblage*, Oxford: Wiley Blackwell.

Perry, B. and Atherton, M. (2017) 'Beyond critique: the value of co-production in realising just cities?', *Local Environment*, 22(Sup1): 36–51.

Perry, B., Durose, C. and Richardson, L. with the Action Research Collective (2019) *How can we Govern Cities Differently? The Promise and Practices of Co-Production. Project Report*, Greater Manchester, Creative Concern.

Piketty, T. (2013) *Capital in the Twenty-First Century*, Cambridge, MA: Harvard University Press.

Richardson, L., Durose, C. and Perry, B. (2019) 'Moving towards hybridity in causal explanation: the example of citizen participation', *Social Policy and Administration*, 53(2): 265–78.

Russell, B. (2019) 'Beyond the local trap: new municipalism and the rise of the fearless cities', *Antipode*, 51(3): 989–1010.

UN-Habitat (United Nations Human Settlements Programme) (2016) *New Urban Agenda*, New York, NY: United Nations.

Simon, D., Palmer, H., Riise, J., Smit, W. and Valencia, S. (2018) 'The challenges of transdisciplinary knowledge production: from unilocal to comparative research', *Environment & Urbanization*, 30(2): 481–500.

EIGHT

Assessment: learning between theory and practice

David Simon, Henrietta Palmer and Jan Riise

Progress in undertaking comparative transdisciplinary co-production

All international comparative urban research is complex and challenging. Hence, attempting to undertake it in countries situated in different regions, particularly bearing in mind the many structural differences and inequalities between the global North and South (as very loose and diverse categories), adds another challenge since relative priorities may differ considerably. For example, in relation to food supply and security, reducing obstacles for informal urban and peri-urban producers and retailers and dealing with the implications of supermarketisation are priority issues in the Southern countries where Mistra Urban Futures has city platforms, whereas the priority issues in the Northern countries centre on enhancing local production of healthy food and reducing the consumption of unhealthy foods, as well as cutting transportation distances and hence food miles and associated emissions.

The challenges are amplified when the global comparative research is undertaken using transdisciplinary co-production (used in this book as a short-hand term that includes co-design and co-creation) rather than conventional academic research teams that to a greater or lesser extent share epistemological and methodological understandings, despite often profound differences between disciplines and in institutional, resourcing and local contextual circumstances, practices and power relations. As reflected in the preceding chapters assessing the pioneering efforts in this regard, transdisciplinary co-production teams seeking to compare locally defined and appropriate projects and research processes within the same research theme in each participating Local Interaction Platform (LIP) face several additional internal and external challenges. Some of these reflect the locally specific nature of transdisciplinarity in each LIP, while others pertain to possible differences in the numbers of partners undertaking the co-production, the particular methods used, differences in the nature of the respective empirical projects, and both interpersonal and interinstitutional power differentials within and across the respective research teams. This does not nullify the value of such comparative research or imply that the challenges outweigh the benefits of such endeavours. Rather, it merely requires a different approach, focusing on making explicit and understanding the different perspectives and methodologies in different contexts, and incorporating them into the respective research processes and outputs. The respective chapter author teams have reflected on these issues in order to add richness to their accounts and provide guidance to others who might attempt such research in future.

The many dimensions of diversity addressed in all the research projects and initiatives reported here preclude simplistic generalisation by way of conclusions. Indeed, that would do nobody any favours. Instead, in the spirit of Mistra Urban Futures' transdisciplinary comparative working ethos, we seek to extend current research boundaries by exploring how far it is meaningful to generalise in identifying principles and guidelines of good practice as part of the research legacy.

Hence, in attempting to distil the current state of play from the diverse experiences encapsulated in the research reported in this volume, we conclude in the final section by suggesting five distinct but overlapping categories of challenge and opportunity in undertaking comparative urban transdisciplinary co-production research, comprising various combinations of internal and external elements. First, however, we synthesise the principal findings and key messages emerging from the respective chapters and the categories of comparative research reflected on in each of them, and how they relate to our strategic objective of promoting equitable and sustainable cities through the Realising Just Cities framework.

Key messages from the comparative projects

In keeping with the approach adopted throughout the book, we focus here on the methodological rather than empirical findings that emerged in the chapters on the respective categories of comparative projects in the typology presented in Chapter Two. The empirical findings are being published elsewhere. It should also be borne in mind that, despite the initial intention to do so, it did not prove practicable to include all the comparative projects in the assessments undertaken by the respective chapter author teams. However, nothing in our experience of numerous project workshops, the formative evaluations or regular cross-platform dialogues leads us to believe that this reduces the validity or value of the findings presented in this book, even if the overall richness and diversity of experience has perforce been somewhat reduced. Moreover, it is encouraging that the formative evaluations and reflective work undertaken by each project team and those using each category of comparison conclude in broadly positive terms about the experience.

One set of challenges faced pretty well universally arose from individual personalities and idiosyncrasies pertaining to the particular context or project, and the very real challenges in setting up the comparative dimensions, especially when these were launched after the commencement of the respective local projects to be compared. Hence, relative timing was crucial, but, in the context of Mistra Urban Futures, largely unavoidable because many of the local projects had origins predating the inception of comparative research in the second phase of research from 2016 onwards. The significance of this issue varied, but was by definition not an issue in relation to the centrally designed but locally implemented project on engagement with and implementation of the Sustainable Development Goals (SDGs) and New Urban Agenda (NUA) (see Chapter Six), despite involving all five city LIPs and two new partnerships established in Buenos Aires and Shimla specifically for participation in this project. The same is true of the Participatory Cities and Realising Just Cities comparative reflexive learning processes, which have not depended on empirical local research – even though for reasons of practicability, the processes conveyed in Chapter Six did not include the Gothenburg side of the SMLIP–GOLIP process. This chapter also underlines the value of different forms of participatory transdisciplinary learning, beyond the types of co-production reported in the other chapters.

The comparative retrofitting project on Solid Waste Management reported in Chapter Three demonstrated the potential for mutual or bidirectional learning between teams in Kisumu, Kenya and Helsingborg, Sweden, despite the dramatic differences in contexts and existing SWM systems. Although it is difficult, for obvious reasons, to generalise on the basis of a single project, part of the power of the experience lay in the unexpected, with the perhaps implicit anticipation of a high-tech Northern approach being recommended for a global Southern situation with which it has little in common. Instead, a very different and more locally appropriate approach has been recommended and is now awaiting institutional approval and hopefully implementation. The transdisciplinary nature of the team was important, bringing different forms of knowledge to the table, and with the basis of mutual respect providing the basis for negotiating an outcome very different from the straightforward yet simplistic and demonstrably problematic recommendation of Kisumu following in Helsingborg's footsteps as some had anticipated. Significantly, too, the team played with and reflected on the dual meanings of retrofitting in this context, and found that the idea of retrofitting a solid waste management approach to a profoundly deficient existing system resonated with the category of retrofitting a comparative project on to a local one.

The three different project experiences of replicating a pre-existing local project in one or more of the other city platforms compared and contrasted in Chapter Four were also broadly positive. The comparative richness shines through and demonstrates the flexibility of the category in accommodating such diversity, because no attempt was made to standardise the projects falling into this category. These represented a spectrum from fairly standard comparative project in the case of Transport and Sustainable Development to something more akin to emulation than replication in respect of the knowledge exchange project in view of the different context in Skåne. Nevertheless, a key ingredient for the eventual success in all three cases – and, indeed, in all the comparative projects regardless of category in our typology – was to build in an initial ideas phase where aims, objectives, research questions and a sense of common purpose were developed. That phase facilitated smoother and more rapid subsequent progress. Perhaps because of the greater similarities of what is being compared in the respective cities, the authors also conclude that this form of comparative project seems easier and perhaps quicker to set up than some of the others.

Chapter Five explores in detail the very reflexive formative stages of what is hoped to become a rich base for future research on migration and urban development. As part of the projects involved had already started before the comparative endeavour, and had other motivations for research, the comparative ambition of the work was, through clustering, to build a knowledge alliance and a conceptual framework useful for all the ongoing research projects in order to produce the embryo of a theoretical contribution to the discourse of urban justice. Indeed, through the formation of a knowledge alliance, the clustering produced new research inquiries on tourism and multi-culturalism that, in turn, led to a successful research bid for a longer research programme on the topic, further developing both the conceptual framework and the collaborations further.

The comparative project on engagement with and implementation of the SDGs and NUA, which forms the subject of Chapter Six, is the only such centrally designed and locally implemented example within the project portfolio. The design may have been relatively straightforward, but the challenge of building teams among academics, non-governmental organisations and local authorities, and establishing the requisite relations of trust within a short time in such diverse contexts, was far from easy. Indeed, the authors document clearly how challenging it often was to identify and establish working relations with the most appropriate officials, and how political dynamics, both with respect to electoral or appointment cycles, and often hierarchical relationships within and between municipal departments, caused delay and uncertainty, with some false starts. Having researchers of suitable experience and sensitivity, and being able to build a very supportive, cross-city project team to provide mutual support, peer-to-peer learning and a sense of shared purpose was also crucial. Indeed, the mutual learning dimension proved important to gaining the collaboration of top officials and politicians, since this was perceived to provide substantive and tangible benefits to the respective local authorities. The same applies to the feedback to and from UN-Habitat and United Nations Department of Economic and Social Affairs in terms of sharing updates and good practice.

Finally, and recalling that one category in the typology, namely the full comparative research by a mobile team of researchers all spending periods of time in each participating city, has not been represented in the project portfolio, and also that projects emerged with their particular characteristics spontaneously rather than by design, the evidence presented has validated the typology as a whole. Most projects fitted readily into one or other category, although one or two had features of two categories and their allocation seemed somewhat arbitrary. That said, the typology is intended only as a heuristic device rather than having any normative content, so usefulness is the only test.

Implications for Realising Just Cities

'Who owns and benefits from comparison and how this enables action on the ground are key challenges for those involved in co-produced research.' This reflection, posed by the authors in framing Chapter Seven, applies equally well to the full endeavour of Mistra Urban Futures' comparative co-produced work. If the rationale behind comparative urbanism has changed from a normative stance in the early 1970s towards a genuine investigation into urban differences, as discussed in Chapter Two, the motivation for comparison in our case is to be found in contributions to realising a more just city through acknowledging and engaging with contextual differences. Diversity, as one governing principle of urban justice according to Susan Fainstein (2014), is increasingly challenged in a current urban condition shaped by processes of both integration and marketisation, pushing towards homogenisation and standardisation of identities as well as of the built environment. Hence, the benefits of comparative co-produced research would need a double purpose, namely to address the multiple teams of local actors involved and to make sense for both their daily practices and their aspirations for a just urban development in their respective local contexts. At the same time, they have to motivate for a level of engagement beyond the immediate, exploring a narrative of urban justice as accommodating diversity and differences, also when such a narrative points towards contradictions and contestations, to counter any single or simplified response to what is sustainable development.

The Realising Just Cities framework, adopted by Mistra Urban Futures in 2016, defined urban justice within three social conditions – ecological, cultural and spatial. The comparative projects emerged and were constructed in responses to these three conditions, addressing a wide range of topics framing urban justice through diverse lenses such as transport, waste management and migration, and within the different organisational set-ups represented in the respective typological categories. The methodological and organisational approaches reported in these chapters have also generated outcomes such as cross-cultural learnings and translations from one context to another, together with cross-context network effects. Importantly, these are acknowledged in all of the projects as results contributing to a deeper understanding of the complexities of urban justice and to a shared engagement in the meta-level of the discourse of how to imagine and realise just cities. Clearly, the substantive issues also affect the organisational set-ups in different ways as the research has proceeded over time, conducing different methodological experiences depending on research inquiry. In this way, research focus and ways to organise around it become interdependent, leading to outcomes as result of both.

Comparing as 'learning through differences', as Colin McFarlane puts it (2010: 728), is central to this endeavour, and our contribution to how to realise just cities. Would it be possible then to distinguish how a certain category of comparative co-production has promoted an investigation of difference in response to the realisation of urban justice, beyond the effects of comparative learning and cross-context networks? Since many of the cases presented are single comparative experiments (the exception is Chapter Four on replication), suggestions should be considered as reflections and possible lines of thoughts to be explored further.

Chapter Three discusses retrofitting as a model for comparison of practices of waste treatment, where the processes of retrofitting take place cross a Kenyan–Swedish context. This could be the typical set-up for a standard technological transfer from North to South. But the discussion of retrofitting is first framed as contextual adaptations in relation to both socio-spatial conditions and modes of governance. Second, it is put into practice in such a manner as to reverse the mono-directional knowledge transfer inherent in retrofitting, by expanding the knowledge production to include sites of material experimentation, benefitting both contexts. The differences of the two urban situations – in technology, practices and governance models – also challenge the established and formalised practices of the Swedish case. The model of retrofitting as it was adapted contributed to a dialogue of balanced differences, where experimentation was offered for mutual benefits.

Chapter Four explores three different research foci of food, transport and formalised knowledge exchange programmes, with the gaze of replication and three explicit and different methods for how replication could be practised. The very different social-economic conditions underlying the first two thematic foci added a tension to the quantitative and qualitative take of replication. In the case of the latter regarding food and food production, the recognition of differences among the four participating cities from global North and South defined four commonly held positionalities that became a tool to expose and question assumed universal stands and values regarding justice and sustainability by identifying the different positions, priorities and values. More profoundly, they facilitated the identification of non-negotiable and shared areas of concern, as a new terrain for investigation of urban justice through the lens of food.

This resembles the strategies evolving from clustering (Chapter Five), where an initial acknowledgement of differences was the driver to carve out a set of themes that could hold differences in a manner that made sense to all and that became productive for each research case individually. However, where the food framework had defined substantive themes, these themes were of a more conceptual nature, defined as transformative. A further exploration into these themes uncovered concepts of 'in-between situations', as different 'trans-conditions'. These concepts, the authors argue, are in themselves directives to realisation of justice – to deal with realities of both, and in terms of multiple belongings, roles and languages, and to actively engage with these in practices of planning and integration.

In Chapter Six, describing an internationally initiated project with local co-production, a framework including different parameters of urban justice was already set by the topic of investigation, as the SDGs and the NUA partly point towards fair and just development. However, as the research topics were extensive and partly elusive, delimitations inevitably became necessary. The contested matter of housing becoming one of these sub-themes highlights how tangibility rather than abstraction provides a 'boundary object', making both the implementation of the SDGs and a cross-context comparative co-production of the implementations possible.[1] This category, as comprising the largest project covered in the book, both in terms of number of participants and funding, also struggled with the greatest diversity of local planning practices and ambitions for implementation. The set-up in itself was possibly the greatest contribution to urban justice as it triggered engagement in the SDGs across a large number of cities.

Finally, Chapter Seven, the opening sentence of which is reproduced at the beginning of this section, shows that, in engaging a diverse set of stakeholders, comparative co-production has the capacity to influence real-life practices and policy making in a very direct and hands-on manner. This is one of the strengths of co-produced research in general, but in the comparative situation described, the addition of a deliberate reflexive moment deepened the public stakeholders' ability to reflect on the practice of urban justice by acknowledging the various differences at play.

In total, these short reflections point towards different ways to arrange research around difference, but also different ways to understand how, by detecting differences, new points of departure, held in common, can emerge.

Challenges and opportunities in taking forward transdisciplinary comparative co-production research

It has been important to think reflexively about the lessons learnt from the complex research processes in the various different thematic areas, how they complement one another and ultimately contribute to achieving more just (equitable) and sustainable cities. This has been valuable as an input to periodic formative evaluation as our research has progressed, in order to provide feedback to colleagues and improve the ongoing processes and hopefully thus outputs and outcomes. It is worth pointing out in this context that no appropriate quality monitoring and evaluation (QME) framework could be found to help evaluate the Mistra Urban Futures' activities and impact. Indeed, conventional frameworks are geared to short-term reporting, as required by many research funding organisations, and usually contain quantitative biases in terms of annual indicators of outputs and turnover that are not appropriate to the complexities and uncertainties of transdisciplinary co-production processes. Indeed, to use such a framework would have been counterproductive. Accordingly, we invested considerable time and effort in developing a bespoke QME framework comprising five complementary elements, of which formative evaluation is one. As a whole, the framework embraces what are widely referred to as first-, second- and third-order effects or impacts. The first order involves direct project-related effects; the second order relates to the immediate context of the project, such as participating institutions and their localities, both during and shortly after the project itself; while the third order constitutes wider societal effects – which are more indirect, removed from the immediate project context and timeframe. These are also subject to diverse influences and are more complex to discern and measure (Williams, 2017; Lux et al, 2019; Williams and Robinson, 2020). The framework has now been tested robustly and is being reported on in separate publications as a contribution by Mistra Urban Futures to the literature on evaluation methodologies (see Mistra Urban Futures, 2019; Palmer et al, 2019).

In closing this volume, our more specific reflections on the diverse comparative transdisciplinary co-production projects and initiatives have led us to distinguish five key elements requiring explicit consideration and sometimes considerable effort to address in view of the complexities and institutional and even very personal sensitivities involved. Accordingly, anyone undertaking a similar project in future should be aware of these and build them into the project design from the outset, with ongoing monitoring for the duration.

- *Project narratives and priorities.* While the different projects in the participating LIPs have matched each other thematically, their empirical foci often differed and they might have had different origins. While in some cases, cross-platform comparison formed part of the logic from the start, in others, comparative work was not part of the initial project narrative. It occasionally proved difficult in rewriting the project rationale to motivate participants to undertake this expanded mission. Comparative work inevitably adds to overall complexity and effort, for benefits that may be uncertain, especially in terms of feedback and tangible local gains. At the same time, the empirical foci and methodologies in one platform or project sometimes served as inspiration in another and formed the basis of the comparison and hence enhanced mutual benefit.

- *Time.* Time constraints increase in complexity and extent when many partners are involved in one location, and even more for international comparative research. Academic, public sector, civil society and private sector partners operate with different calendars, budget cycles, time pressures and degrees of flexibility over their timetables. In a North–South or other interregional comparative context, differences in annual calendars, workloads, salary levels, facilities and infrastructure, and performance and assessment criteria can prove challenging both for the same kinds of stakeholders and across stakeholder groups. For instance, collective teamwork between Swedish and Kenyan PhD students was hampered by such differences, with the Kenyans having to juggle research and thesis writing on top of full-time academic posts, while Swedish students were able to devote far more of their working time to their studies (see also Simon et al, 2003; Palmer and Walasek, 2016; Darby, 2017). Setting up clear and realistic goals that can adapt to local constraints, as well as planning in advance the expected times for engagement between the international partners, may not eliminate these challenges but may reduce misunderstandings and facilitate collaboration.

- *Funding.* Different funding sources have different durations, stipulations about the extent of paid employment required or permitted, and demands on results. While common co-funding from a large multi-year programme, such as Mistra Urban Futures, is invaluable in enabling work on a common agenda, it cannot fully overcome the kinds of often-sharp differences outlined in these paragraphs. The contemporary requirements by funders and some host institutions to demonstrate direct downstream or societal impact within specific timeframes are particularly challenging in inter- and transdisciplinary sustainability research (Simon et al, 2003).

- *Culture and power.* Cultures of decision making (hierarchies, traditions, gender relations, levels of formal educational attainment, attitudes to age differences and the like) and communication (formal and interpersonal communication, different forms of knowledge, methods of interpretation and ways of knowing, the ability and willingness to have a voice in research team discussions) differ considerably across and within large institutions, countries and regions. Indeed, these dimensions are intertwined, complex, and often implicit and subtle, making actual change difficult to engender in practice, even when all agree it is appropriate (Palmer and Walasek, 2016; Darby, 2017; Perry et al, 2018). Yet failure to bridge such differences could reduce the value and quality of both the outputs and processes of mutual learning. These differences require careful and respectful exploration, discussion and resolution, with mindfulness of asymmetrical power relations. Beyond these principles of good practice, and making use of any institutional codes of ethics, anti-discrimination and harassment policies and the like, there is no simple toolkit for addressing such entrenched and often emotive issues. If all else fails, existing complaints procedures have to be used as frequently and strongly as possible as a way to address issues.
- *Governance.* The outputs and outcomes of transdisciplinary comparative work are subject to expectations of different kinds, based not only on the actual setups of the respective projects themselves, but also on the relevant governance structures of the participating organisations and institutions in each platform. The same work may be assessed very differently when the focus is usability in the local context, or analytical depth and diversity. To address this concern, research teams may need to produce outputs and interventions in different formats for the respective institutions and audiences, both in any one location and across the research locations. As explained previously, such diverse requirements and expectations should therefore

also be factored into an appropriately designed QME framework.

All of this underscores the importance of effective ongoing engagement throughout each project's life in order to address the different needs and priorities of the often-diverse participating organisations. The professional and personal engagement of each member of each research team is key to understanding the outcomes and potential impact; the differences are not seen as obstacles, but are the very stipulation for success. This engagement is also crucial to maximising effective external communication and to sharing and disseminating outputs and outcomes to different stakeholder groups and audiences, from the local to the global. It is also worth noting that the communication efforts tend to include recommendations, as in policy briefs, and suggestions for action. This is a development from 'science communication' in its traditional form towards more advocacy and activist-oriented communication (see, for instance, Davis et al, 2018).

Finally, it is worth reiterating that transdisciplinarity, in the sense deployed here of different sectors or stakeholder groups working together in various participatory and co-productive ways to generate new research and knowledge for mutual benefit, sometimes still seems 'off the radar' to many academics and other communities of practice. However, interest in and demand for it are increasing rapidly in the face of the limitations of conventional expert-led and hierarchical processes and conflictual relations between different urban stakeholder groups. There is still much work to be done to ensure that transdisciplinarity is fully recognised and accommodated within urban (and all) research funding mechanisms, academic evaluation and promotion criteria, public sector procedures, civil society organisational senses of legitimacy, and private firms' willingness to engage on the basis of shared intellectual property rights. It is thus heartening that while current advocacy for a distinctive and academically interdisciplinary 'urban science' could be seen as pushing in the opposite direction, the recent authoritative report *Science and the Future of Cities* recognises the importance of engaging fully with all other categories of actors:

> Communities, NGOs, citizens, consultancies, international organizations, city networks are all involved in the production of information and knowledge that, to varying degrees but of certain global presence, now fundamentally shapes urban development. Rather than dismissing these actors as 'un-scientific', the urban science community needs to think its role and position in relation to those players. An agenda for engagement, advocacy, training, and rebalancing emerges here... (IEPSFC, 2018: 33)

The work reported and reflected on here therefore truly extends the frontiers of urban research and knowledge production, and we hope that it inspires and assists others to push further.

Note

[1] This is the opposite of what happened in Chapter Five.

References

Darby, S. (2017) 'Making space for co-produced research "impact": learning from a participatory action research case study', *Area*, 49(2): 230–7.

Davis, L., Fähnrich, B., Nepote, A.C., Riedlinger, M. and Trench, B. (2018) 'Environmental communication and science communication – conversations, connections and collaborations', *Environmental Communication*, 12(4), 431–7. doi: 10.1080/17524032.2018.1436082

Fainstein, S. (2014) 'The just city', *International Journal of Urban Sciences*, 18(1): 1–18. doi: 10.1080/12265934.2013.834643

IEPSFC (International Expert Panel of Science and the Future of Cities) (2018) *Science and the Future of Cities*, London and Melbourne: IEPSFC. Available from: www.nature.com/documents/Science_and_the_future_of_cities.pdf

Lux, A., Schäfer, M., Bergmann, M., Jahn, T., Marg, O., Nagy, E., Ransiek, A.-C. and Theiler, L. (2019) 'Societal effects of transdisciplinary sustainability research – how can they be strengthened during the research process?', *Environmental Science and Policy*, 101: 183–91.

McFarlane, C. (2010) 'The comparative city: knowledge, learning, urbanism', *International Journal of Urban and Regional Research*, 34(4): 725–42. doi: 10.1111/j.1468–2427.2010.00917.x

Mistra Urban Futures (2019) *Mistra Urban Futures Progress Report 2016–2019*, Gothenburg: Mistra Urban Futures. Available from: www.mistraurbanfutures.org/en/news-and-media/annual-report

Palmer, H. and Walasek, H. (eds) (2016) *Co-Production in Action*, Gothenburg: Mistra Urban Futures. Available from: www.mistraurbanfutures.org/en/annual-conference/conference-book

Palmer, H., Polk, M. and Simon, D. (2019) 'Evaluative and enabling infrastructures: supporting the ability of urban co-production processes to contribute to societal change', Paper presented at the International Transdisciplinary Conference 2019, University of Gothenburg, 12 September; under review.

Perry, B., Patel, Z., Norén Bretzer, Y. and Polk, M. (2018) 'Organising for co-production: local interaction platforms for urban sustainability', *Politics and Governance*, 6(1): 189–98. doi: 10.17645/pag.v6i1.1228

Simon, D., McGregor, D., Nsiah-Gyabaah, K. and Thompson, D. (2003) 'Poverty elimination, North–South research collaboration and the politics of participatory development', *Development in Practice*, 13(1): 40–56.

Williams, S. (2017) *Evaluating Societal Effects of Transdisciplinary Co-Production Processes. Final Report to Mistra Urban Futures*, Gothenburg: Mistra Urban Futures. Available from: www.mistraurbanfutures.org/en/publication/evaluating-societal-impact-transdisciplinary-co-production-processes

Williams, S. and Robinson, J. (2020) 'Measuring sustainability: an evaluation framework for sustainability transition experiments', *Environmental Science and Policy*, 103: 58–66.

Index